I0213947

Written Words from a Grateful Heart

Martha Lloyd Cooke

Ideas into Books ®
WESTVIEW
Kingston Springs, Tennessee

All recipes in this book are used at *Martha's Tea House & Memories* in Murfreesboro, TN.

Ideas into Books®
W E S T V I E W
P.O. Box 605
Kingston Springs, TN 37082
www.publishedbywestview.com

Copyright © 2020 Martha Lloyd Cooke
All rights reserved, including the right to reproduction, storage, transmittal, or retrieval, in whole or in part in any form.

ISBN 978-1-62880-193-4

First edition, February 2020

Printed in the United States of America on acid free paper.

Contents

Written Words from a Grateful Heart is dedicated to my mother and father. Neither of them could read or write, but they both worked very hard and sacrificed all for their four children. I am their oldest daughter.

Johnnie and Mable South

Life on the Farm
Eddie and Martha's Story

After 112 years of Cooke Family ownership of River Bend Farm, Murfreesboro, Tennessee, there is a wedding in the house. The original home burned in 1969 and Aunt Sarah Belle Cooke rebuilt a new home in 1985. After her death the farm was purchased by a member of the family, Eddie Buford Cooke, Jr. This is where the story begins.

Eddie Buford Cooke Jr. and Martha Lloyd Cooke were married in the dining room of the home with several family members and close friends present. Our small wedding was filled with love and happiness that continues to grow even stronger today.

We have enjoyed working on the many projects in and around the farm. New flooring, appliances, painting, and bathrooms were completed first. The driveway was gravel but was quickly replaced with an asphalt drive. On a farm there is always work to be done. Many changes have been made through the years but the charm, peace, and beauty always remain to be enjoyed by family and friends.

A guest house was converted into Martha's Tea House where all her Bible study and book club friends enjoy tea parties and lunch quite often. The Tea House is painted many bright colors and adorned with many memorable items from past experiences. Peace, love, and solace surely abound in this Tea House.

A few weddings have taken place in the middle of the pasture under the big oak tree. Hay bales were used as seating for all the guests. The receptions are under a big white tent in the pasture by the house. The oversized patio serves as a dance floor with a disk jockey spinning favorite songs. Everyone always has a good time.

Eddie and I enjoy our home, farm, family, and many friends. The farm is so beautiful and peaceful. The comfortable home has a welcoming spirit. We call it our "Little Piece of Heaven."

Eddie and Martha Cooke

January, 2015

I often hear people talk about their bucket list of occurrences they would love to experience before giving up life as we know it today. Much of the time the list is too long or too complicated and we lose interest in trying to accomplish what seems to be impossible. One such thing on my bucket list was a hot air balloon ride. I didn't really think I would be brave enough to even try and conquer this feat. Not much thought went into making this real. Just thinking about it gave me heart palpitations!

On September 1, 2012 we had a farm wedding. The young couple had a beautiful wedding on our 117-year-old farm. The wedding was complete with one hundred hay bales for guest seating in the middle of the pasture under a big oak tree. Two hundred guests attended and most were from out of town. The rehearsal and reception were enjoyed by all. The disc jockey played all the favorite songs and the dancing began. As they say, "It was a blast," the way a wedding should be.

We did not expect any compensation but the night of the reception, the beautiful couple presented a gift certificate to us for a hot air balloon ride. I immediately thought they had wasted their money! The certificate was good for one year, thank goodness! Eddie and I did not think too much about it for several months but in July, 2013 we knew we had to make that dreadful decision to experience this phenomenon. We were going to do this! I contacted Smokey Mountain Hot Air Balloon and scheduled this flight for September. The balloon is owned and operated by Captain Jack and Gina Wheeler who live in Murfreesboro. Captain Jack has been a captain with a major airline for twenty years. That made me feel a little better, I think. His wife, Gina, is a lovely lady who actually does the navigating of the balloon from the ground. A family affair they have been executing (Gosh, I don't really mean "executing" ☺) performing for twenty years. They have three daughters and one son.

With wheels in motion I started making plans for a party in the pasture for family and friends. The balloon would accommodate four people plus Captain Jack so we invited two of our best friends, Linda and Wilson, to fly with us. (If we were going down then they were going down with us!) I prepared lots of food, drinks and a "bucket" load of champagne (one whole bottle for me ☺). Neighbors came from all around, including children to watch the affair. The deflated balloon arrived on a special trailer and was placed in the middle of the pasture by one of the barns. The sunny day was perfect for this adventure. The balloon inflation was a family, friends, and neighbors undertaking (did I say undertaking!) task. The elevated excitement by everyone, including the children, was at its peak! (The bottle of champagne wasn't bad either). The photographer was snapping pictures of everyone, even after we ascended into never-never land (I meant to say the beautiful blue sky!).

The voyage lasted approximately two hours. We floated over 2,000 feet above the earth and then low enough at one time to pull leaves from the tree tops and talk to curious viewers on the ground. The landing was so smooth. Gina and her family met us with a bottle of champagne, (just what I needed!) After a brief ceremony we were presented a certificate of completion for a happy, fun hot air balloon ride. So glad we did this!

Do you have a Bucket List? Be careful what you place on that magic list. You never know what you can experience! A hot air balloon ride is not for everyone. I certainly did not think leaving the earth in this manner (did I say that!) was for me either.

This bucket list adventure was one of the most exciting and fun happenings I have ever experienced. Make sure you have a bucket list and enjoy this life.

Martha, Eddie, Linda, and Wilson

January 20, 2016

Big or little we all have happy times or have experienced settings that make us happy just by being in that moment. I have had my share of these special times and once you have been there the memories are etched in your mind forever. These memories can be shared in many ways and I choose to write this one story to be shared with friends and family because of the many blessings my husband and I experienced in Costa Rica.

Recently we had an opportunity to travel to Costa Rica for eight days with dear friends. I immediately thought "I don't want to fly" but it was either fly or give it up for another beach scene close to home. We flew into Liberia, Costa Rica on an early Saturday afternoon (whew!—smooth flight). ☺ We had a forty-five-minute bus ride to the JW Marriott, located by the Pacific Ocean, about twenty miles from Tamarindo, fifty miles from Santa Cruz and feeling like we were in the middle of nowhere! We were only a few miles from Nicaragua which was not too comfortable for me after my husband informed me they had been trying to reclaim this Costa Rican coastline for many years. Several of the hotel employees drive from Nicaragua each day to work.

Walking twenty steps to the ocean each morning and taking a quick swim was a beautiful experience. I found the most interesting shells I have ever collected with unusual shapes and sizes. You could not resist the morning and evening beach walks. Breakfast, lunch, dinner, and everything in between could be served and enjoyed in one of the six dining facilities or just about anywhere you wanted to be at any given time. We enjoyed breakfast on our balcony, lunch by the acre-size pool and treats while sunbathing by the ocean.

We had a couple of days of sun, fun, and relaxing on the beach before we decided to shop and explore Tamarindo, a seaside town located twenty miles away. We quickly discovered this was a surfing village with very limited shopping but lots of hotels. Very few people spoke English. We discovered a restaurant on the beach and enjoyed the seafood and entertainment by a Mariachi band.

Karen and I were not ready to give up on shopping and this is when we discovered that Happy Place. I could continue to talk about all the luxuries at the hotel we enjoyed but let me tell you the real story. Karen and I had such a happy awakening. Eddie and Dave were on a deep sea fishing excursion on Thursday so we traveled by cab to Santa

Cruz for shopping with a chauffeur who spoke both English and Spanish. Karen and I do not speak Spanish so the chauffeur was a must for traveling in rural country. We

traveled for an hour and a half with the chauffeur "presenting" his beautiful country to us. Large cattle farms with beautiful green mountains as high as the sky were all along the route. Robert, the chauffeur, was so proud of his country and he wanted us to be a part of it too. He talked about the culture and described many scenes along the way. He even stopped at some of the homes by the roadside to introduce us to people he knew. Their "castles" were small and crudely built and they were so proud to share them with us. The yards were actually part of their living area with tables and chairs everywhere. The children and adults were gathered around eating, talking, laughing, and enjoying life.

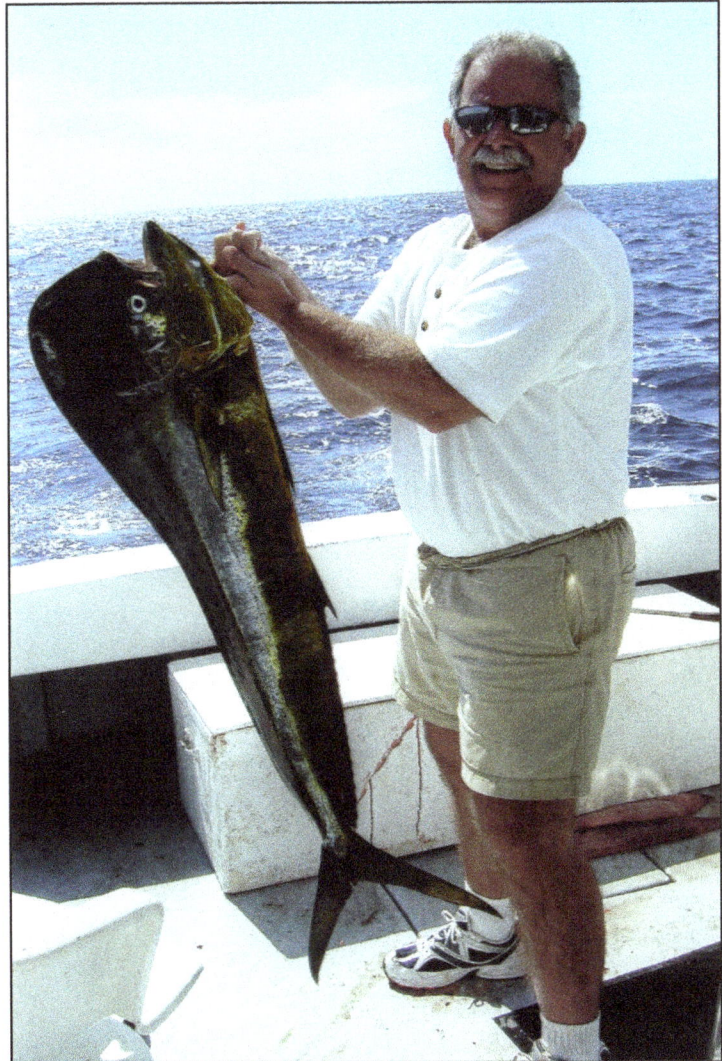

We also stopped at a roadside business that made wooden "Costa Rica" signs and some wooden figurines. Oh my goodness, it is a good thing the lady had only two signs available because Karen and I would have bought fifty of them! She was so friendly and had the most beautiful smile. She was just happy we stopped and didn't really try to sell anything. She was a happy person and content to be in her small three-sided shop with the leaky roof. I took so many pictures of her! I wanted to capture that smile and remember the blessing that Karen and I had received.

We arrived in Santa Cruz and were immediately overwhelmed! Right in the middle of the town is this one-hundred-plus-year-old beautiful Catholic Church with a front door big enough for a school bus to drive through. The doors never close. People were constantly coming to pray as we sat in awe on the back pew. These families have been attending this beautiful church for many generations. Across the street was a small park full of families with children and grandchildren just playing and enjoying this daily routine. They would just smile as I snapped picture after picture. I was so taken by their kindness and relaxed way of life that I didn't want to leave!

We walked into all the little shops along the way and were just amazed. There were no art and craft shops. We were hoping to find quality gift items for family and friends but there were none. In this part of Costa Rica most everything is imported from China and Japan. The shops were filled with walls and racks of children's clothing, shoes, and accessories. The most adorable children were all along the street playing as the adults supervised and cared for them. It all appeared to be one big happy family, loving and caring for one another. After a short three hours we had to reluctantly depart from this peaceful happy setting. On the trip back to the hotel we asked Robert what was most important in his life. He replied, "loving family and friends, experiencing happiness, and just enjoying life."

The loving, happy little town of Santa Cruz and Robert's philosophy on life really were an awakening for me. Why can't we, the American Families, enjoy a simple life, love family and friends, and experience true happiness? We are busy—with what? We don't know, isn't that a shame! Life is meant to be simple and happiness has to start from within. Restore your faith, love your family and friends, and really enjoy life. Experience a Costa Rican moment, slow down! Find your Happy Place! Take the time to clean out the "upstairs" in your life and ask for a little help from the Lord, He is always there.

"Rejoice in the Lord always."

Philippians 4:4

Welcome to America, Crawley Family! We don't have a Georgian Country House and we don't have to be concerned about the Titanic sinking around here. Our Downton Abbey story originates on a country farm of fifty acres with a ranch style home and a charming Tea Room experienced and appreciated by many ladies. I must share a story about a recent celebration that you would be pleased to have attended.

The ladies in our "Not Your Ordinary Book Club" are avid followers of your Downton Abbey drama. One of our members, Glenda, just celebrated her 50th birthday. Glenda thought it would be a great idea to have a Downton Abbey Birthday Party in the Tea Room on the farm with all the ladies dressed in proper British attire. March 10th, 2018, at 12:30 PM the fun started. A toast to the Birthday Lady and "The Downton Abbey Strut" began! Mary, Edith, and Sybil would have been proud of the beautiful garb displayed. Abounding and unique "Crawley" hats and hairdos and beautiful dresses of all colors including royal blue, ruby red, and white lace were on display. Even the butlers, Paul and Dennis, in their tuxedos, did a great job by always appearing promptly at the ringing of the bell. Even though these two handsome men did an outstanding job they are not for hire. Paul is the husband of Glenda and Dennis is the husband of Carmenann, book club members. Sue, the unique and creative baker of the group, designed a beautiful specialty strawberry birthday cake for Glenda depicting the magic of the day and capturing a few British moments. Yes, the lighted candles were extinguished on the first try.

The Tea Room has four tables with chairs that seat twenty people. The tables are always dressed in different designs depicting a holiday or any special event for any of my friends. Two sofas, a chair, artwork, and a coffee table located in a slight niche of the main dining area are always welcoming for tea and conversation. Bring one or six friends, "prop" up your feet, and enjoy the afternoon in this relaxed and welcoming area. Could it be nap time?

The walls are full of "Martha Memories," ranging from a 1959 wedding dress to a thimble and tea pot collection. Look closely or you will miss the baby dress worn by her sister Sherry who is now fifty-eight years old and the baby sweater and shoes that belonged to Carol, Martha's daughter, who is now forty-seven years old. Do you like dolls? Ask Martha to tell you about Elizabeth, Cozette and Lollie Corine who reign over the Tea Room. The ceilings are 4' x 8' sheets of plywood that Martha has painted in bright colors of red, purple, yellow, and green. One of the windows is adorned with her husband's Tabasco ties while another features teacup placemats. You cannot miss the special hot air balloon stained glass displayed in an opening between the Tea Room and kitchen area.

So much more I could tell you about my Little Piece of Heaven" but maybe you need to come and do your "strut" in "Martha's Tea House with Memories." The Downton Abbey affair was unique and so much fun! I consider it a blessing to be a part of the "Not Your Ordinary Book Club" and to share the friendship, good times...and books!

Brunch Punch

1 (46 ounce) can pineapple juice

3 cups orange juice

2 cups cranberry juice

¾ cup powdered sugar

¼ cup lime juice

Garnishes: lime or lemon slices, fresh mint leaves, cranberries

Stir together first 5 ingredients, cover and chill 2 hours. Stir before serving. Garnish if desired. Juices can be chilled before mixing the punch to eliminate refrigerator time.

Makes about 3 quarts.

The Downton Abbey
Birthday Ladies

1   pound cut up or coarsely ground crawfish tails

1   large onion, chopped

4   tablespoons crawfish fat

½   cup seasoned bread crumbs

1   egg, beaten

Double crust for 9-inch pie

2   ribs celery, chopped

Salt, red pepper, black pepper (to taste)

2   cloves garlic, minced

¼   cup chopped green onions

¼   cup chopped parsley

½   cup butter

½   cup bell pepper

1   cup whipping cream

Heat whipping cream. Add celery and crawfish fat, and let simmer 5 minutes.

In separate pot, heat butter and add onions, garlic and bell pepper. Sauté until limp. Add cream mixture, green onions, crawfish, and parsley. Simmer 10 minutes. Remove from heat and add bread crumbs and egg. Salt and pepper to taste.

Pour mixture into pie crust. Place second pie crust on top and make two or three 1" knife slits in the top crust for ventilation. Bake 10 minutes at 450 degrees. Reduce heat to 350 degrees and cook another 35 minutes or until crust is golden brown.

Glenda is a Nola Girl who left Louisiana and relocated in Tennessee. She enjoys cooking, sewing, painting, and especially tea parties. Glenda is always entertaining her many friends and her home is always open to anyone who needs a helping hand. Her Louisiana home style is charming, interesting, and unique. She always makes one feel right at home. Makes me happy to call her my beautiful friend.

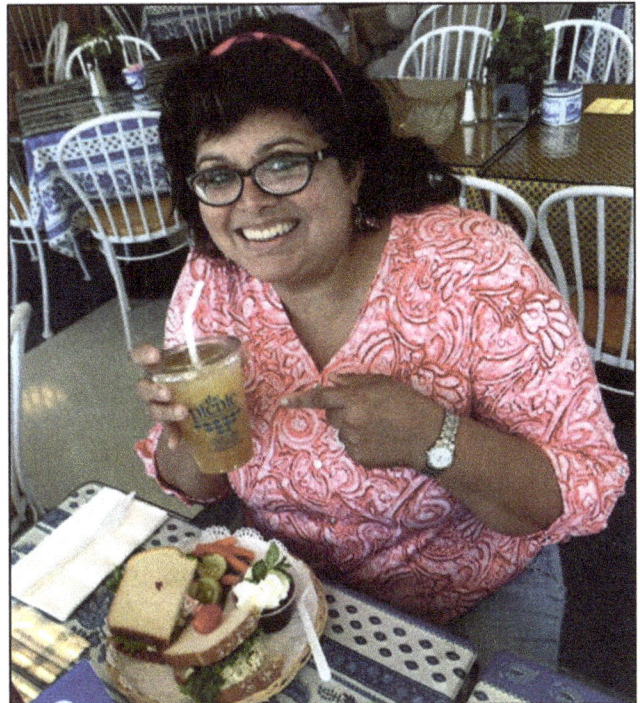

December 1, 2015

A forever blue sky, a never-ending white sandy beach, and the gentle rolling waves coaxing your toes into the water as you lie in the sand on your new beach towel. These are only a few of the happy moments one experiences when the beach is in full bloom.

Every year Eddie and I escape to Seaside, Florida by ourselves at Thanksgiving. We leave the Wednesday before Thanksgiving and return home on Sunday evening with a refreshing new feeling and outlook about our lives and our loved ones. When you escape to a vacation getaway you find an appreciation for the small things in life and a realization that this life is not a rehearsal so do your very best to spread love and kindness and be the person that the Lord has mapped out for you.

The place we rent is truly one of a kind. We were late making a reservation in 2013, but there was a cancellation and that is how we discovered this condo. This one-bedroom, 1500-square-feet dwelling has so many first-class amenities. The owners live in this Conservatory part time. A library is located in the bedroom with just about any kind of book you would ever want to read. If you don't read but like to play the piano then the baby grand piano sits in the dining area on the third floor. There is a private elevator and also a spiral staircase that goes from the main living quarters to the roof where the hot tub is located. The bathroom is equipped with a steam bath and oversized whirlpool bathtub. The artwork reflects scenes from all around the world and is truly one-of-a-kind. We don't usually stay in any place like this when we vacation so don't get the wrong idea about us. We are just "common folk"! I thought you might like to hear about its uniqueness. One more thing happens, a Christmas Parade! On Saturday afternoon Santa and Mrs. Claus ride in the parade in a horse-drawn carriage. They greet the children with candy and there is visitation time with Santa. The Christmas lights come on in the middle of "Seaside Square" and Christmas bells are ringing. Such a happy time is enjoyed by all.

Friday we get to the beach early for a day of sunshine and long walks. You see all kinds of people walking along the water edge. Then there are people who gather on the beach in groups to play with their children. I began to observe the people walking and I wondered what their lives were like. One particular lady came by walking very briskly wearing a T shirt that read "I can and I will." I gained inspiration from this instance just thinking she might be working toward conquering a special sickness or just trying to be a healthier and happier human being. Everyone has a story. That quote inspired me to look at some of the things in my life that I know I can change for the better.

Next to us were a group of people who had several children. The father of one little girl decided she did not need a bathing suit so he removed the suit and let her remain naked on the beach for over two hours. She would wander away from the group then the parent would go find her, bring her back, and let her sit in the sand and play with the other children who were dressed in bathing suits and cover ups. This incident was very hard for us to understand. It made us think about children that are abused and seemingly nothing being done about it. Be the best parent you can be to a child who is only on loan to you for such a short time.

Seaside, Florida, is a place where bicycles and pedestrians rule. Sometimes more bicycles than people, but it all works very harmoniously. There are bicycle trails everywhere that take you to interesting places, such as Water Colors where all the homes are painted in beautiful pastel colors. Shopping is fun and you can always find something unique and different. This beach resort is a happy place. If you are not happy when you get here then you will find happiness before you leave!

October 3, 2014

"Here she comes —Miss America." Starting in 1955 and continuing through 1979, Mr. Parks sang this song to introduce the new Miss America to the world each year. This ceremony usually takes place the first Saturday evening after Labor Day. In these early years our family was one of the few blessed with a television so we were glued to this television set in our living room for this event of the year. Each of our family members, neighbors, and friends selected his/her favorite beautiful lady to be the winner of this gala affair. All the contestants were so lovely that we hardly ever chose the winner but what fun we had guessing! The traditional Miss America Pageant has continued every year since 1979 with a different person presenting his rendition of the Miss America melody. Burt Parks will always be my favorite.

Have you ever thought about what goes into the making of a Miss America pageant? The rehearsals, makeup, hair, and forever smiles are just a small part. Glenda, our book club leader, thought it would be a great idea to have a Miss America party at her home. Everyone would be dressing in evening gowns, wearing a tiara, having dinner, and watching the televised event on September 14, 2014. I got nervous and excited just thinking about it. As the week of the party unfolded, I started putting my attire together for the big event. I knew I had the dress and shoes but I didn't know about a tiara and all the other accessories. By Friday I was so excited about being a part of such an event I was telling everyone. My husband surprised me with a new tiara and helped glue the "MISS ARKANSAS" letters on my red shoulder sash. I was chauffeured to Glenda's home for the special event. When I arrived I could not believe how beautiful all these ladies were. There were dresses of many colors: black, red, purple, aqua, and burgundy. We looked like the Miss America pageant! Everyone was having such a good time.

Glenda had an abundance of food, complete with a cake. Paul, Glenda's husband, helped to make the party special with food preparation and all the ladies expressed appreciation. A party is not complete without pictures and the camera was rolling. One of the ladies brought a camera with tripod for really good pictures. Thanks also to Glenda's son, Alex, who volunteered to be the patient photographer. Eleven ladies and a 5th grade little lady, can you imagine just right pictures of everyone? We missed our friend, Penny, who recently had thyroid surgery. Our prayers were with her.

Before the pageant started we had to select five states which we thought would be possibilities for Miss America. Carmenann had chosen the winner, Miss New York, who has won for the past three years. I was glad that my home state of Arkansas was one of the top five. This finale called for a champagne celebration and more pictures. We had so much fun we decided to make this an annual event.

With all the beautiful ladies present we had our own beauty pageant with everyone winning! Beauty is more than skin deep and these friends represent the very best in the beauty of this world. Preparing for this party really made me stop and think about the mad, crazy world a beauty contestant experiences.

Thank you Glenda for your creativity and generosity!

Rolling pastures, winding half-mile-long driveway alongside the Stones River, frolicking deer, and three barns waiting to be explored are the perfect setting for a day of surprises. With the sunshine, enthusiasm, and excitement no one seemed to notice the forty-degree temperature. The fifty-acre farm was purchased in 1896 by the Robert Cooke Family. The farm is surrounded by the Stones River on three sides. Eddie and Martha Cooke are the present farm owners who live, play and enjoy sharing this little piece of heaven with friends, family and neighbors.

Today is a day for sharing with friends. My friend, Glenda, and I had talked about her and the family coming out for a walking tour and target-shooting experience. Eddie prepared the location for target practice and the fun began when Glenda, Paul, Alex, Glenda's mom, and Alex's friends arrived. Today is December 29, 2018, 1030 AM. Such an exciting group of friends and everyone was ready to walk. Our first stop was the wedding tree in the middle of the pasture where you can still hear the "I Do" echoing from the weddings performed under this tree. The three barns are all different and were built over a seventy-five-year period. My favorite of the three is located in the wedding tree area and has been used many times for beautiful wedding scene photography. We walked around the barn while I shared the history of this sightly structure. Aunt Sarah Bell Cooke loved herding her cattle to this barn every afternoon for feeding and enjoying the cattle conversation of the day.

We continued on for a glance at the oldest barn located closest to the Stones River which meanders approximately two hundred feet below the farm property. The third barn was the charm when I opened the door to reveal the big, beautiful green John Deere tractor reigning over the whole building. I could tell the nine-year-old really was excited about the tractor. She climbed into the big seat like she had done this a hundred times before and her dad snapped the memorable picture.

Next we joined Eddie in the pasture for some target practice. The day was brisk, bright, sunny, and perfect for honing gun skills. Everyone was ready to participate in this fun event. Glenda even took a shot at the elusive little orange target. I said everyone but Glenda's mom and I decided to watch from a safe distance and escape the loud noise. These "gun totin" men finally worked up an appetite. We headed to the house for a robust breakfast celebration, a cup of tea, conversation, and my Hummingbird Cake for dessert.

Amazing how quickly time flees! What seemed like only a few minutes was actually over three hours. Paul, Glenda, Alex, and Glenda's mom have been our friends for several years. You never know with Glenda who you will meet next. Eddie and I are grateful for all our friends. Please come back to our farm, our home, our little piece of heaven. There is always something new to explore and a tea party in Martha's Tea House would be fun. Baby dolls are always special guests.

"This is the day which the Lord hath made; rejoice and be glad in it."

Psalm 118:24

August 15, 2017

I have told this story to many friends and family. It doesn't matter how many times I tell it the same facial expressions appear and you can see the fear and surprise in his/her eyes. These things never happen to us. You just read or hear about it on the news. Occasionally when I think about this incident it seems unreal to me. Always be aware, cautious, and alert, especially at home. I was a victim of a home invasion in the middle of the afternoon.

We live on a farm one-half-mile off the main road on a private one-lane asphalt drive next to the Stones River. I stay very busy doing projects around the house. This day, February 28, 2012 was no different than my usual routine. At 1:30 PM I took a short break to relax on the sofa in the TV room located next to the sunroom. At 2:00 PM I heard a knock at the door but I was not expecting anyone so I did not go to the door. Five minutes later there were two men looking through the windows. Two more minutes and a window was being opened in the sunroom. I knew they were coming in! I walked to the far end of our home and secured a gun located in our bedroom. On the way to the bedroom I picked up the telephone to discover the line had been cut! After securing the gun I positioned it in my hands and walked back to the TV room. I saw one man depositing my accessories into a huge sack. I and the gun laser made eye contact with this criminal. He and his partner scrambled to get out of the damaged window. At this point I stood and watched them escape behind one of the barns in the back of our home. I had lost all energy at this point so I never fired a shot. Using my cell phone I called my husband Eddie and the police who were on the scene within ten minutes. Later a picture lineup was presented to me and there he was! The police informed me they had been looking for him because he had just been released from a ten-year prison sentence and had stolen his uncle's truck. I couldn't identify the second bandit because I had only seen him from a distance and he had on heavy clothing and wore a cap. The two culprits had walked a trail by the river and came up around the barns located in back of our home.

These two thieves lived in this area. Both men were apprehended and one was imprisoned again. I was recently informed of the release of this prisoner. I would know him anywhere but I hope I never have to see him again.

I have become really efficient with firearms and I tell people I shoot first and ask questions later. The police told me I made one mistake—I should have shot him while he was in my home. I'm not saying I am the bravest but I try to be aware, cautious, and alert at home or any other location. Don't take anything for granted. Had I not owned a gun at that time who knows whether I would be here today to tell you of this personal scary experience.

Thank you Jesus for protecting me and our home!

Pasta–Veggie Pie

Recipe suggests 2 quart deep dish or 2 quart Lasagna pan when baking.

Two ready- made pie crust (I use Pillsbury-2 in a box that unroll)
7 ounces linguine
Veggies: red pepper, broccoli, onions, mushrooms, or other favorites, and garlic
Olive oil, Parmesan cheese and/or chicken breast cut into pieces.

Sautee veggies and/or chicken in olive oil then drain. Cook linguine as directed and drain.

Coat dish with oil and sprinkle generously with cheese. Lay crust in dish. Mix linguine, veggies and/or chicken and spread into the deep dish. Place second crust on top and sprinkle with parmesan cheese. Bake at 350 degrees for 30 minutes or until toasty. Let cool 15 minutes.

January 6, 2017

On a trip to New York a few years ago for shopping and theatre, I purchased a beautiful strand of pearls. The pearls are medium sized and 24" in length. Through the years these pearls have brought so much enjoyment, not only to me but a few friends who have borrowed them for their wedding day. I sometimes place them in a spot on my dresser for viewing and reminiscing as I saunter through my bedroom many times each day. Each time I look at these pearls I recall many special memories.

Life is full of treasures and often hard to find because we are too distracted to take notice of the real pearls of life. Most often we hold these pearls of life just in our hands rather than storing in our hearts. Life is like pearls, placed on a string one at a time in all sizes, shapes, and colors. The Number One biggest, brightest, and most important pearl on this string is the Gift of Life which takes center stage. I was twenty-nine years old when my only child, Carol Ann, was born. The birth of a child is humbling and can be overwhelming to know God has put his trust in you to nurture and love his baby angel. Guard this gracious gift of life and the beginning of your beautiful strand of pearls.

I have pearls for my Mother and Daddy that are placed close to the center of my pearl necklace. My Daddy passed in 1985 and my Mother joined him on March 18, 2016. My Mother loved pearls and Daddy was one of her brightest pearls. Mother was 95+ when she ascended to Heaven and her strand of pearls was long, bright, worn, and ready to present to the Lord. She had experienced the gift of life in some amazing ways and looked forward to placing that last pearl of joy in Heaven with Daddy.

Sometimes you just have to place extra pearls on the string for some people or life experiences. I have only one child, Carol Ann, who has always amazed me with her accomplishments in life. She is a role model and mentor and loves coaching and choreographing award-winning cheerleading and dance teams. She also holds the position of Spirit Coordinator, University of Memphis. I could fill a complete strand of pearls that represent my love and respect for her.

Pearls are everywhere if you just take the time to recognize and cherish. My husband, Eddie, is one such pearl that is irreplaceable in my pearls of life. He is always supportive, understanding, and a great strength for me. Eddie is a Mortgage Banker working very hard helping people with home loans or giving to anyone who needs a helping hand.

Through the years I have known or worked with all sizes of pearls. They sometimes come when you least expect them. Have you not recognized your many pearls? We all have them. Open your heart and mind and take the time to load your Strand of Life Pearls. Happiness does come in small packages and helps to form the abundant life you are promised.

I'm not finished with this "Pearl Thing"! I look every day for new ones to add. The hunt is exciting, brings me joy, and enriches my life. I pray that "my load of pearls" is pleasing to the Lord.

"Open your Heart to All that God has planned for YOU."

"The Lord will fulfill his purpose for me."

Psalms 138:8

4   family size tea bags
1   12-ounce can frozen orange juice concentrate
1   12-ounce can frozen lemonade concentrate
1   cup sugar

Bring tea bags to a boil in 3 cups water, remove tea bags, add sugar and stir until dissolved. Pour tea and sugar mixture into a gallon container. Add thawed orange and lemonade concentrates. Fill remainder of container with water and stir.

Our Bible study shared the tea and the recipe with me, a real treasure. I serve at all my tea parties.

February 22, 2019

John Henry South, seventy-two years old, passed into Heaven on February 27, 1985. This day was normal with no anticipation of any happening, especially saying hello to God in the late afternoon. Johnnie was just sitting in his easy chair, fussing at Mother because she was sick and did not want to go to the doctor. Heart failure in his favorite chair at home was the culprit and it was quick. How often do you hear stories like this? Too often but — but — but I didn't get to say goodbye. Not one second of time is promised to anyone so you have to throw away the "but" and do what God wants you to do, LOVE and HONOR your Mother, Father, and family. Heartache touches all of us in this heartbreaking and phenomenal world today. The question is "What does one do to contend with heartache, disappointment and sadness?" As Charles Stanley says, "The dark moments of our life will last only so long as is necessary for God to accomplish his purpose in us." No Christian has to go it alone. No Jesus — then know Jesus.

No sadness with this story because we had a Happy Daddy. Everything he did was for the betterment of his family. Wearing his overalls and heavy work shoes every day and working in his garage made him happy. I could walk into the garage and he would want me to come listen to a car he was working on. The car was running so smoothly and he was so happy that he had pleased the owner of the car and made me smile too.

Happiness to Daddy was watching wrestling on Saturday night, eating cornbread in milk, and enjoying a glass of his famous iced tea. When anyone visited he always brought out the tea and smiled so proudly when the compliments started. A special little pitcher in my cabinet was used to take tea or ice water to the garage during long hot days and the smile was always there to show his appreciation. Some nights all he wanted to eat for supper was a big glass of milk with Mother's homemade cornbread. Wrestling was very real to my Daddy. Saturday night, 10:00 PM and he and I would be in front of the television with Daddy making almost every move the wrestlers made. Some of it was funny and he would laugh but you never told him any of it was a fake; those were fighting words.

Things I remember that made my Daddy smile: Seeing the joy on our faces while unwrapping Christmas presents on Christmas morning, Daddy opening the Christmas box that always had a new pair of overalls, and peeling oranges and apples for us to eat after we opened all our gifts. Christmas was his favorite holiday and we shared the day, Mother's cakes, and our love with many aunts and uncles.

See, this story does not end here. My Daddy was such a Happy Daddy and enjoyed the simple life. He cherished his family, always worked hard, never complained, and always wanted to do the right thing. My Dad had a second-grade education so he did many things with a handshake because he believed people were good.

We miss the unforgettable HAPPY DADDY SMILE. He is forever in our hearts. Take a really good look at your loved ones. They have secrets they don't even know they have. Look closely, you can discover those smiles and happy moments that can fill a book.

"Believe—Nothing is impossible with God."

Luke 1:37

April 13, 2018 - Friday the 13th

April 4th, 1968 Martin Luther King, Jr., evangelist, was assassinated while delivering a speech from the balcony of the Lorraine Hotel in downtown Memphis, Tennessee. I was also downtown Memphis on that date. A friend and I were attending classes at the downtown location of the University of Tennessee. We quickly hurried home to West Memphis.

April 4th, 2018, the 50th anniversary of the Martin Luther King, Jr. assassination I was downtown Memphis again. The hustle and bustle for the fifty-year celebration was in full swing. Streets were blocked, speeches were being scheduled everywhere, especially at the Lorraine Hotel, and people were marching. A policeman was on most every corner. I was in route to West Memphis, Arkansas to pick up Carol's wedding invitations. I mapped out a route to cross the old Mississippi River bridge in order to miss the congestion of the celebration. As I traveled on this journey all these memories came flooding back into my heart and head. I am seventy-five-years-old now, and I remember that dark, sad period in our American history. Today as a result of this tragedy great progress has been made on discrimination.

After I secured the wedding invitations I decided to stop by Howard's Donuts for a few treats. Daddy always loved this place and their special glazed treats. I decided to buy a few of these treats and travel to Marion, six miles down Interstate 55, to Crittenden Memorial Park

Cemetery. I knew Mother and Daddy were resting in peace and I wanted to create a new memory with them. Upon arrival I walked around for a few minutes then I removed the donuts from the box. I got my camera and snapped several pictures of their graves, Johnnie and Mable South, and also the grave of Alvin Lloyd (Carol's father).

The whole time I was there I was talking to Mother and Daddy and enjoying the donuts. All of a sudden I got this idea. I could stand next to Mother and Daddy's gravesite and my shadow would be cast over half their tombstone so it would look like the three of us would be enjoying that Howard's donut together. It worked! I experienced such a peace and as I left I told them I would be back soon. Howard's Donuts are habit forming and who better to share one with!

Crazy little story? Well, maybe, but the joy and peace I felt is unmatchable. Let your heart breathe, be creative. Listen and look for the special moments in your life. We all have them. Share one with a friend or relative just like I have done here. There is a memory or blessing around every corner if you just look, listen or imagine.

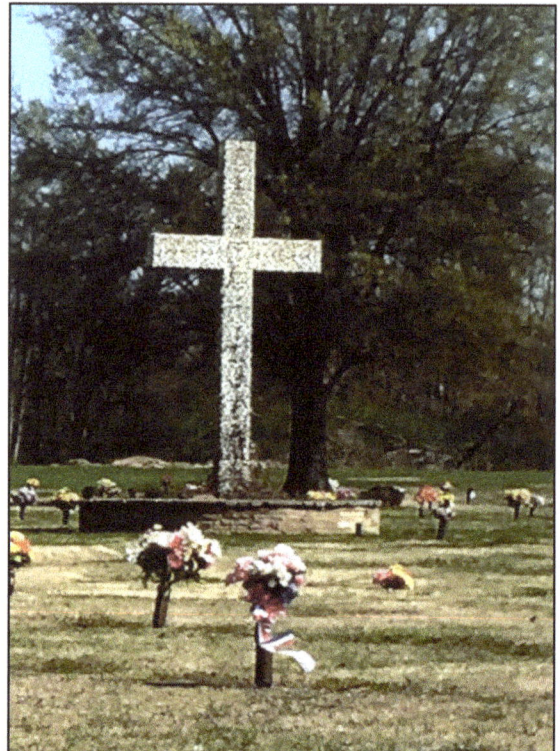

Johnnie and Mable South Gravesite.

"You can talk to God any time because He's listening all the time."

"Call upon me and pray to me and I will hear you."

Jeremiah 29:12

November 26, 2018

Oh Lord, how the time does fly! Only yesterday Daddy was walking me through his garden, located out by the cotton field next to our home in Joiner, Arkansas. While carefully directing me to his big beautiful red tomatoes, hearty pole beans, and vibrantly yellow squash, he always had the cutest, proudest grin on his face. I knew what was coming next. Daddy loved preparing and sharing a cool glass of his sweet iced tea and always had a big full pitcher just waiting for us to enjoy after touring his garden and pulling a few weeds. The front porch swing was the perfect setting for tea time, just the two of us. We could have sat for hours but Daddy was a self-employed mechanic in his shop located next to our home which supported a family of six, so our time together was limited. Sometimes I would follow him into the shop to the nearest car, truck, tractor, or school bus and hand wrenches to him as he worked so we could talk a little longer.

Hours, days, weeks, months, and years I shared with my Mom. When I was a little girl I always wanted to do "big girl" things. Mother washed our clothes in a big black iron pot in the backyard. She used a small board with ridges in it on which she rubbed the clothes clean, rinsed and then hung on a wire clothesline until dry. You guessed it, I loved helping with the laundry! The washing of the clothes was fun, but I begged Mother to allow me to do the ironing. I would cry until she finally set up the ironing board and flat iron, stand me on a stool and I would iron all our clothes. Being the oldest of three children at age seven, I was taught many household chores and worked with my Mom on all sorts of projects. A big four-layer yellow cake made from scratch with red jelly icing would not be perfect today without my Mother's shared secret ingredient, LOVE.

I had no idea where I was going with this story on a cold gloomy fall day. As I was sitting and enjoying a cup of hot tea I spotted a group of deer out our bedroom window. A family of seven deer was frolicking in the pasture between the wedding tree and barn, which I see quite often. This morning was different. Today is the Monday after Thanksgiving. My thoughts were of our family and wishing we could all be together out there under the big wedding tree being happy and sharing our family love.

The conundrum of life is hard to understand, especially when we are young. I remember a quote on the wall of the Home Economics building when I was in the 9th grade at Shawnee High School in Joiner, Arkansas, 1957. It talked about youth being such a wonderful thing and a shame it is wasted on young people. I felt disbelief and confusion that someone would say such a thing about us. The meaning is very simple. We know nothing other than basic needs when born. As we grow in our life experiences of success, failure, laughter, tears, peaks, and valleys, we have learned to be brave, spend the last little time we have to practice what we learned when we were young. Faith, kindness, patience, forgiveness, and the greatest of all, LOVE, should abound.

I appreciate the fresh start I experienced with my life. Without the guidance of a strong Christian Mother and Daddy where would I be today?

"Love bears all things, believes all things, hopes all things and endures all things."

I Corinthians 13:7

Do you have one? Are you missing the importance of this miracle? Are you caring and respecting it in the way that is intended? This miracle is called the "River of Life" and you surely have received this gift from our Lord Jesus Christ. Every human being has their own river to cross. How do you treat your personal river? Do you jump in with both feet immediately or are you taking life's river one day at a time?

I recently wrote a story about a river, the Mississippi. My Mother and Daddy were baptized in this river when they were in their 60s. They had been experiencing their river for many years, challenging years, good times, and some not-so-good, but knowing the journey to the other side meant being "Home at Last." Mother and Daddy took this slow walk into the river and renewed their faith in this gift of life.

Having your own river and making life decisions can be very challenging, but isn't life great! You may have your almost-perfect life but is it really perfect? When that almost-perfect life is disrupted by many consequences such as separation of family members, sickness, death, or your faith in Christ, how do you continue to journey to the other side of the river? Do you rush into the water making all the quick decisions for everyone involved? (Which are usually wrong!) Or do you approach this river with a slow walk and receive the blessings, your blessings, in these deeper healing waters?

Sometimes this river journey seems so hard we want to just give up in the middle of it, swim back to shore, and forget the whole process. I have a problem with this thought—I don't swim! I'm on my way, over half-way now, and I'm not going back. I trust Jesus that He will not let me drown in my river and you know, I can vaguely see the far side of the river, Home. I'm not perfect, just forgiven.

Where are you in your River's journey? Treat it with love, understanding, compassion, and forgiveness. It took me a long time to discover that I even had my own River of Life. But once you have that talk with Jesus Christ, ask for forgiveness, and follow Him, then you are on your way. Start Swimming!

My Mother passed on March 18, 2016, ninety-six years old, and she was a strong swimmer in this world called life. She always told us "You don't miss your water until the well runs dry." Don't wait too long because the well will run dry. I learned so much from her and some of it was the hard way. I loved her so much.

July 9, 2018

Oh my goodness, I cannot believe she told that about me! We have been friends for several years and this fabrication did not sound like anything this friend would ever utter. The lie spread to several people but the most important was my husband. The hurt I felt was too much for me! My husband confronted this person and she finally admitted that everything she spoke was heresy and false. Yes, I was terribly hurt when I heard the lie but then I allowed the ugly anger to take over my heart, my head, and my complete composure. I don't even remember everything I said to my husband but the words were spoken which created many unpleasant moments. The devil laughed, the Lord was saddened, and I cried. My reaction was not the right behavior of any Christian. What had happened? I was so disappointed in myself. Has it ever happened to you? I would venture to say YES! Let me talk to you.

Are you a chocolate chip? My sister Carolyn and I talk every day about many subjects and she shared a story with me about these sweet chocolate morsels. First of all chocolate chip cookies are one of my favorite to bake. After listening to her talk about these cookies I had a greater appreciation for the significance of the chocolate chip. After gathering all the required ingredients for blending, mixing, and baking, the process starts. The flour is blended with the sugar, eggs, vanilla, salt, baking powder, and milk or whatever your recipe requires. Next comes the most delectable and favorite part of all, the chocolate chips to make the batter complete. You have blended all the ingredients and notice you can't really tell one ingredient from another except the chocolate chips. These little jewels stand alone. They do not lose their shape, size, or color but they mix, not blend, with the cookie dough to be perfectly baked for all to enjoy.

Let me ask again, are you a chocolate chip? Have you "blended" and become unidentifiable or have you chosen to be "mixed" and recognizable to the world? Being in the mix means to stand alone and be the person God has created you to be, a beautiful and unique human being marching through your life fully dressed in your armor.

Be the chocolate chips in the cookie dough of life. Keep your form and remain completely intact and distinct for the world to see. Sometimes we fall prey to being blended and lose our identity. Prayer is the easiest thing to help you get back to the mix, it can work wonders!

What a Great Batch of Cookies we can all be! Get started today, this moment. After all, moments are all any of us have in this universe.

"Lord, after this life experience I know you have made me a stronger and better person. Thank you for helping me one more time to understand and appreciate You and your love."

You have filled my heart with GREATER JOY."

Psalm 4:7

My Friend, Bobbi Bryant's Spaghetti Salad

1 pound spaghetti
1 cucumber
1 green pepper
1 tomato, chopped
1 red onion
½ bottle McCormick Salad Seasoning
1 (8 oz.) bottle Italian Salad Dressing

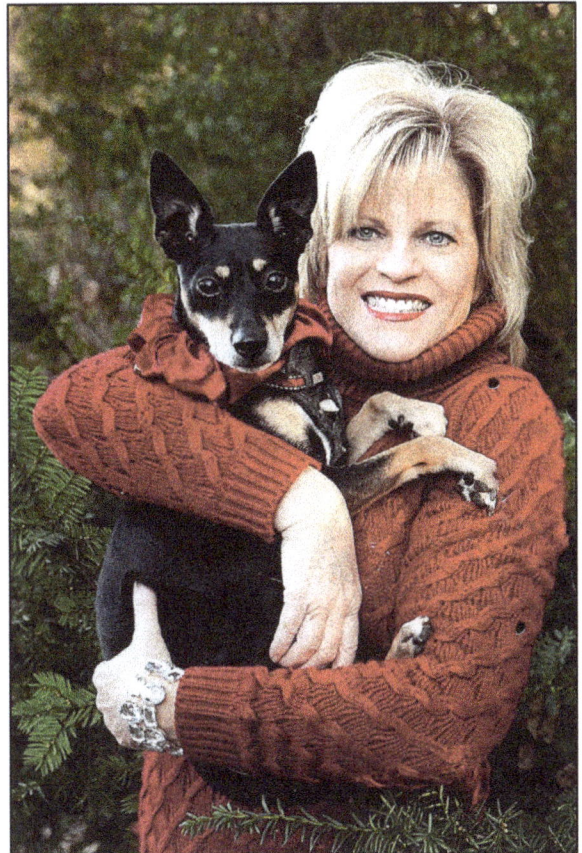

Cook spaghetti until a little chewy. While still hot, mix with all ingredients. Store in refrigerator overnight before serving.

If I told you I liked fishing then I would have to inform you that I just told a whopper. Fishing has never been of any interest to me. In 1952, when I was nine years old, I experienced fishing one time with Aunt Bertha and Uncle Tom and knew it was not for me. Fishing with a cane pole and squeezing the worms on the fish hook sounded gross to me. We sat on the bank by the pond with baited fishing pole in hand and waiting and waiting for some dumb little fish to eat the worm so we could catch him for our dinner. I had rather been in my playhouse or making mud pies. Sometimes the wait was long so while waiting for the little scaly creature to fall prey to the baited hook you had to practice quietness and stillness. Quietness and stillness are not my best attributes. Pesky mosquitoes, baking sun, thirst, starvation, and no singing or playing forced me to return to the house and wait for the fishermen to come home with the catch.

We have traveled to Cabo San Lucas, Mexico many times and my husband enjoys deep sea fishing. He leaves early morning and returns about 2:00 PM. One year we were fortunate enough to bring 200 pounds of Mahi Mahi home with us. I accompanied him on one excursion but not to fish. After a short while I realized I was going to be trapped on this fishing boat in the middle of the ocean in the hot sun for hours. The waves were rolling and my stomach was rolling with every wave. Fishing in the Pacific Ocean in Mexico is an exciting adventure for fishermen who love to fish but I don't like fishing.

I do realize there are variations of catching that fish. A lot depends on the amount of money one wishes to spend for equipment which sometimes includes a boat and a vehicle for transportation to the fishing hole. Or maybe you live in an area where everyday life means daily fishing in order to have food and income for your family. Well, you can tell by now I don't know much about catching that fish. I'll leave that to the experts.

My form of fishing is happening all over the world. Anyone can do it and I am an avid supporter. "Dropping the nets" and searching for people who do not know the Lord. We should be witnessing every day to the friends, family, or anyone who does not know of the power and freedom that can be released into their hearts and souls. Your heart is full of joy and is meant to be shared with all people. I have always believed one should never cease praying. Step out your front door and you are on the mission field. Let your light shine and use your gift of prayer by praying with humility for anyone who needs to experience the love of Jesus Christ. I recently read that we have God's assurance that He hears and cares about every prayer, even the prayers that slip down our cheeks as silent prayers.

The mission field is waiting! Isaiah 49:16 states "See, I have engraved you on the palms of my hands; your walls are ever before me." With the death of Jesus Christ all our sins have been forgiven. Looking at the palms of my hands is a constant reminder of God's love for his people. We must be diligent! Pray for guidance and drop those nets while we have the opportunity. Let's find those lost, hungry fish and bring them home to Jesus Christ. Amen!

1 box Lemon Supreme cake mix
½ cup sugar
²/₃ cup oil
4 eggs
1 cup apricot nectar (found in juice aisle)

Mix ingredients, pour into greased-floured bundt pan. Bake at 350 degrees for 30-35 minutes or until golden brown on top. I have used orange, strawberry, banana and pineapple cake mixes and the cake is very moist and delicious. I usually let the cake set about 5 minutes in the pan before removing to cake platter.

GLAZE: Mix small amount powdered sugar with apricot nectar until you get desired consistency then spoon or pour over the cake. Or you can serve cake without the glaze, excellent either way.

My Bible study friend, Janet, shared this special recipe with me a long time ago. You would have to know Janet, she does it all. Seven grandchildren, ages three to sixteen, are her delight. She paints beautiful pictures for friends and family. I have a hot air balloon picture she painted especially for me and I cherish this art. She always seems to know exactly what people like. Janet also sews, making all kinds of crafts for her grandchildren and friends. If you need a special friend then you must meet Janet.

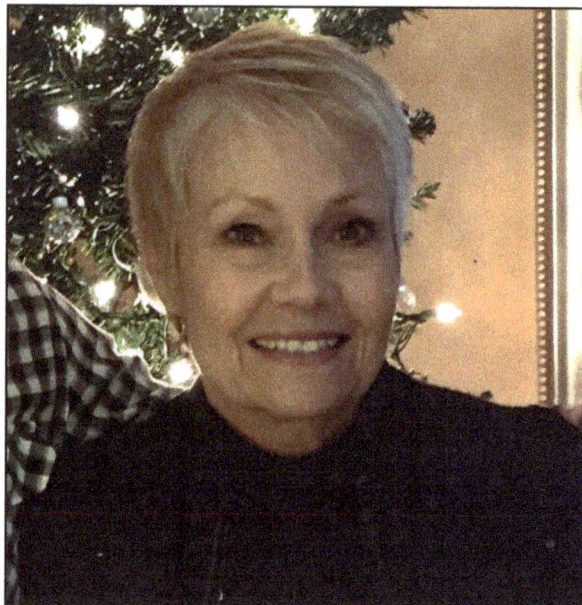

December 23, 2017

The time has finally come and I must do it now. Why have I waited so long? I think about it a lot but I seem to find so many more interesting endeavors to occupy my wandering mind. When visiting friends or relatives I observe the same situation or predicament as I have. I create this quandary because I fail to take the time to do the right thing. You probably know what I am talking about by now. But, then again, you could be like my little sister, Sherry, and have a place for everything and everything in its place. She could get up at midnight, march through her home and find anything she wanted without even a flashlight. She and her husband, Joe, are very active members of their son's church, New Life, in Jackson, Tennessee. Clothes, shoes, umbrellas, keys, hats, books—you name it, a place for everything. On the other hand, I am totally opposite. My closets and drawers are full of unwanted and unnecessary items. I have too much of everything, like most people, that needs to go, but it's our stuff and it's a form of security. One can always do that chore tomorrow, which seems to never come. Well, the time has come at my house. I started emptying out drawers and closets last week and I rediscovered my spacious home. I have some friends and my nephew's church that have shared some of my priceless stuff.

Does all of this sound ridiculous? Yes, we have clutter in our homes but have you ever stopped to think about the clutter, confusion, and disorder we have in our spiritual life? Certain situations seem unbearable so we just busy ourselves loading up the closets and corners of our mind and life without the Lord's help. Wham! It hits like a ton of bricks! We suffer the consequences of a "do-it-yourself fix." Regretful thoughts flood our heart, mind and body. We realize that God's way is the only way. All we have to do is call upon the Lord, admit our mistakes, and ask for forgiveness. You can start immediately cleaning out the corners of your life by praying and asking for guidance.

Will you make more mistakes, take a wrong turn, pile up your life closets, and lose the boundaries of your life corners? Guaranteed! None of us are perfect; we all fall short of the glory of our Lord. March on and work each hour of the day doing the best you know how, helping other people, and living a Godly life.

I say this quite often. We are not perfect but we are forgiven.

"The steadfast love of the Lord never ceases, his mercies never come to an end. They are new every morning."

Lamentations 3:22-23

Being born and Living in Joiner, Arkansas for eighteen years with my Mother, Daddy, and four siblings, were some of the most unforgettable formative years of my life. We were forty miles from Memphis but only a few miles from the Mississippi River. In those days very few families, if any, had swimming pools. Very often our weekends were spent driving to Thirty-Seven Island for access to the Mississippi for swimming, boating, picnicking, and fishing. Everybody joined us, aunts, uncles, and plenty of cousins, to make it a perfect day of fun and family fellowship. The Mississippi River is the place where we all learned how to swim by just jumping in and figuring it out for ourselves. As children we were not scared and we knew our parents would be our safety net.

I tell you this about our family and the Mississippi River because this old Mississippi contributed to one of the most memorable events in our lives as a family. At the time there is no way you can appreciate a happening such as this. We think we cherish these moments but they become even more special as we age and hopefully become wiser. Let me tell you my story.

Mother and Daddy were members of the Bassett, Arkansas, Pentecostal Church. Bassett was only two miles from our home in Joiner and the church membership was fifty to seventy-five people. I have no idea how old the special little church is, I only know I'm seventy-three years old and the church is still active. Our Mother and Daddy had a special dream and shared the dream with the church members and our family.

Carolyn, Wayne, Sherry, and I were not sure how this would work but the Lord would make a miracle here.

Our Mother and Daddy wanted to be baptized in the Mississippi River! Once we learned of this we put the wheels in motion. Church members as well as the aunts, uncles and children were invited to witness this blessed event. Our parents wanted Brother James, their Pastor, to officiate the event. We chose a beautiful sun-filled Sunday afternoon right on the banks of the Mississippi River. There was prayer and singing then the baptism started. Daddy was first, led into the chest-deep water by one of Mother's brothers and Brother James performed the ritual of baptism. Our Mother was so different. She believed that white clothing should be worn for baptism so she was dressed in white. Mother wore a white blouse and white skirt and marched right into the water as if she were on a white sandy beach in Florida.

The picnic celebration was such fun. Everyone was so happy and our hearts were filled with blessings. There was a cotton field where we parked with a little dirt road. We pulled out our picnic feasts, placed them on the hoods of the cars and pickup truck tailgates to be enjoyed by all. We thanked God for such a hot and dusty day and the miracle we had just witnessed.

I shall never, ever forget this special day. Today when I see cotton fields my thoughts are rekindled. Memories flood my heart and mind of our Mother and Daddy being baptized in such a special way. Pictures really are worth a thousand words. Thank You, Lord, for all you do.

I have a clock I have cherished for many years. This beautiful wooden wall clock is eighteen inches round and embellished with brass surprises in many areas. This special clock reigns over one wall in my living room. A large round pendulum located in the back swings continually on a background of royal blue dressed with musical notes and rainbows. In front of the pendulum is a large brass circular disk that turns displaying small brightly colored clowns with musical instruments that seem to be dancing on a background of musical notes and rainbows. In the numbers area of the clock sit two clowns that are brilliantly attired with flashing lights that are always an eye catcher. When the clock starts performing with a melodious song each hour, there are flashing lights, turning wheels, and bright showy trinkets to watch in amazement. Some of the songs include "Over the Rainbow," I Will Always Love You," and "Beauty and the Beast." There are a total of twelve songs which include six traditional and six Christmas. A button on the side of the clock is used to switch from traditional to Christmas music. I love all the songs. Why not have beautiful Christmas music all year too? When walking through the house you can always hear the music that starts a new hour. I have to stop, listen and think about the many blessings I have, especially family, friends and a home that I love and share with all.

Why did I tell you about my clock? I awoke this morning with my clock playing one of the beautiful songs and I remembered a story about my Daddy. Christmas time was the best at our home! I was twelve years old and it seems like yesterday for this memorable Christmas of 1955. Daddy was always looking for something different to surprise Mother for Christmas. This Christmas was special! We always had a Christmas tree decorated by December first, and the presents would start appearing soon after. There was a gift that made an appearance right in front of the tree so all could see. Daddy had wrapped the gift and it was for Mother. We were not usually allowed to touch the presents but Daddy wanted each of us to hold it and try to guess what was inside. We guessed something different every day but we never got it right. My Daddy was always such a happy fellow and he so enjoyed the scene each day of our hopeless guessing. Mother tried guessing a few times but it always ended with her returning to the kitchen to make a few more homemade cakes for the Christmas crowd.

We never opened Christmas gifts until Christmas morning but by Christmas morning we were all ready to tear into packages and check the Christmas stockings surprises. But, not this Christmas morning, we were all so excited about Mother's gift from Daddy that we had to sit and watch as she opened the special box, a beautiful clock! Our Daddy was ecstatic! He laughed for days about this feat he had just accomplished. In fact, he always showed delight when anyone admired the clock and that was the entire neighborhood. We had never seen anything like this before and Mother was in awe. It stood about sixteen inches tall with the clock face located at the top but the real beauty was located on the bottom half. It was a fireplace! When you plugged in the clock there were lights located in the back of the fireplace that made it look like a real fire! No more touching this gift! This special clock was positioned on top of the television set for many years so we could enjoy its beauty while the family watched television. The little things in life do count. I love this moment. Do you have memorable moments? Share them!

Where Could It Be?

After experiencing anger, anxiety and sheer frustration you ask yourself "Where could it be?" You often search for a particular item until the brain shuts down and there is not another possible hiding place. Considering it gone forever is never a possibility. Don't give up on yourself or the hunt. The mind nudges the seeker to continue the pursuit. I have talked with people who hide heirlooms, money, and many other keepsakes when travel from home is necessary. The problem with this system is that they cannot remember the hiding places when they return. Absent mindedness and attention span can cause real dilemmas when cherished items are not stored in that one special place. Have you ever thought about how much time is used or wasted from searching for everyday items such as eyeglasses, keys, jewelry, shoes, or clothing? Paying attention and proper storing of such items could alleviate some of the frustration, anger, or anxiety that we needlessly experience.

I experience this time-stealing culprit most every day. I have this unique and beautiful silver necklace purchased by my husband for a special occasion. I wear it once or twice a week. It's missing! I just know it is gone forever! I am exhausted and bewildered because I know I placed it in the same box in the same drawer as I have done for the past year. I've looked everywhere I can imagine and the necklace is just not here. I searched for a week before even mentioning it to my husband. Yes, he was upset so he looked every place I had looked but the necklace was not found.

After pondering this loss I really became embarrassed that I had spent so much time looking for such a tangible earthly item. My next feeling was embarrassment. Heaven has much greater rewards. I started praying and asking God for forgiveness. My husband and I didn't think or talk about the necklace for a couple of days.

Sunday morning I was dressing for church and looking for a couple of pieces of jewelry to wear with a special dress. I opened the jewelry drawer to select a necklace. I selected another necklace since my favorite silver necklace was missing. When I gathered up the necklace I planned to wear, there underneath was the special silver necklace which had been misplaced by me. Another prayer for forgiveness was spoken for not trusting.

Yes, we have to trust even in the smallest things. Who needs necklaces, keys, glasses, or any other earthly junk? Don't sweat the small stuff. Keep your eye on Jesus, you can't go wrong living for Him.

1 box Duncan Hines Devil's Food Cake
    Mix
1 small box instant vanilla pudding
3 eggs
1 cup oil
1½ cups buttermilk

    Bake in preheated oven, 350 degrees, for 25-30 minutes.

FROSTING

8 ounces softened cream cheese
4 Hershey bars – grated (save a small
    amount to sprinkle on top of cake)
½ cup sugar
1 cup powdered sugar
16 ounces regular Cool Whip, not lite

    Once cake has cooled, spread frosting on each layer and top of cake. Store in refrigerator for a while before serving.

    Angie is the expert cake baker. She delights everyone in the Bible study with her surprise cake creations. Angie has been my lovely friend for many years and attended many tea parties at my Tea House on the farm.

Sunday morning, August 24, 2014, Eddie and I were in the first service at our church in Murfreesboro, Tennessee. During the praise and worship we were singing a song that had the term "jars of clay." Sometimes I don't hear very well and I thought the phrase was, "jars of day." My thoughts turned to our daily living habits. Our lives should be lived one day at a time but in our busy world today we tend to live days, months, and even years into the future instead of enjoying the present moment.

"Jars of Day" reminded me of my sweet sister-in-law, Sandra, who lives in Pennsville, New Jersey, to whom we had spoken during the week. Every year she makes dozens and dozens of jars of grape jelly from the vines in her yard that their Dad nurtured and cherished during his life time. The jars are pint and one-half-pint size. She sent pictures of the jelly cooking and her filling the jars. She has fun doing this for family and friends and we always have homemade grape jelly in our home. ☺ Last year for a wedding here at our farm Sandra produced two hundred jars of jelly in half-pint jars to give to all the two hundred guests! What a surprise and treat for everyone!

Picture your life in jars, jars of "day." You open a new jar of life each day and there are all kinds of surprises, depending on your mind set. During the years do you sometimes find day jars that have been cracked, broken, mishandled, abused, or the life fruit is already spoiled? Your jars of day have to be handled with special care only by you. Good care brings on a happier and satisfying life.

The jar of the day, the cracked jar, could be a damaged or difficult relationship and you see no solution. Look for ways to redeem difficult situations. "Trusting God's faithfulness helps dispel our fearfulness." The broken jar can be even more heartbreaking, especially when a loved one has gone on to be with our Father in Heaven. The grief can be devastating but with courage and God's intervention we march on in life opening the next jar. "It takes the storm to prove the real shelter."

We don't always make the good or best decision with life situations and we all experience those cracked, broken, mishandled, abused, or spoiled-fruit jar days. The secret is attitude and asking the Lord for help with any situation and acting upon his command. We are not perfect but we are forgiven. Exceed expectations and look for ways to dispense grace in our world.

"Trust in the Lord with all your heart, and do not lean on your own understanding. In all your ways acknowledge Him, and He will make straight your paths."

Proverbs 3:5-6

Click, click, and click some more! Another holiday or special occasion and everyone's cameras appear from nowhere. Those perfect pictures are a photographers dream. One thing for sure we all know is photography is not always great but the beautiful family and friends smiling are a perfect moment. Once these moments are captured what do you do with them? Do they end up reposing in your telephone camera collection until they are deleted to make room for more special moments? We love these pictures but somehow excuses can be found to delete, delete, delete. Always wanting more but never taking time to enjoy the treasured life photos that were captured in the not so distant past. Pictures developed, placed in frames, and displayed for friends and family to enjoy is a real passion of mine. I have these memories displayed in most every room of my home. I started reminiscing about the hundreds of pictures I have taken and decided the time had come to drag out the special picture box from underneath my bed. Here they are, just as I left them six months ago. I always experience happiness, sadness, excitement, bewilderment and sometimes confusion, but by the end of the viewing these memories give satisfaction, joy, and a special peace. The picture box is a real treasure so I decided to share a few of these magic moments with my friends and family.

Our daughter, Carol Ann, started cheerleading in the third grade and continued through high school. She attended college at the University of Memphis where she was a member of the National Champions Dance Team for four years. During the four years, the team traveled extensively which included going to Spain, Italy, and Japan with the NBA. Carol is now the Coach/Choreographer of the National Champions Cheerleading/ Dance teams and Spirit Coordinator for the University of Memphis. Carol also Coaches and Choreographs for Collierville, Tennessee, National Champion Middle School and Varsity Teams. Can you imagine how many photo albums have been filled and I never tire of browsing through each one.

What is your favorite holiday(s)? Easter and Christmas were two of the most special. On Easter morning we all dressed up in our new clothes, went to church and then loaded into the back of Daddy's truck and headed to the Memphis Zoo, forty miles away. Mother always prepared a huge picnic lunch and we always had fried chicken. All six of us would trample through the zoo together observing all the animals. We knew the picnic lunch was waiting so we raced back to the truck to enjoy our Mother's special meal. We hid Easter eggs so many times that we forgot where some of them were even hidden. This Easter outing was such a fun relaxing day for everyone. We have pictures but I wish there were more. Maybe you can picture your Easter moments and enjoy reading about mine.

Cakes, cakes, and more cakes adorned our kitchen table and cabinets. Mother loved baking cakes! Aunts, Uncles, and neighbors all around came to our house for cake at Christmas time. One of my favorites was a four-layer red-jelly cake. Can you picture that? Yellow cake with strawberry jelly slathered between the layers and all over the top, so yummy! Pictures of everyone who visited were always taken in front of the cedar Christmas tree. Presents were piled high and remained unopened until Christmas morning. Eight, ten, twenty people—we never knew how many would appear for Christmas dinner. The door was open to anyone who did not have family or families who just wanted to be with our family. The dinner table extended into the living room and beyond and there was always plenty of food. My one hope is that you are blessed with special Christmas memories and family. Pull out those pictures; they are usually guaranteed laughter and love. That is what life is all about.

Life is not always happy but life is not always sad either. Thank goodness for photographs that can make us laugh at ourselves or just break down and cry when we see reflections of our loved ones who have passed on to a better place. Even with the sad pictures there is always something that conjures up a smile or maybe even a belly laugh. One sad picture of my mother comes to mind. Three years before her passing she fell and suffered a brain bleed. While in the hospital we thought she was hallucinating. She was seeing and talking to angels. Little angel children were appearing and she was talking to them and trying to touch the angels but they would disappear. We laughed and agreed with her as we watched her reaching with outstretched arms and hands and when they disappeared she would become very angry. Who knows, maybe angels were in the room protecting her. This picture of her in the hospital bed with family all around thinking the time had come is very special. One of those few times all our family was together. Sad but true that it often takes a sickness or death for families to come together. But look at the happiness and celebration of a newborn baby's birth and families coming together to celebrate this magnificent miracle. Everybody wants to hold a newborn baby and everybody has a name suggestion. Click, click, click go the cameras! Get the photo albums ready!

I hope by writing this story it will inspire you to pull, drag, or crawl to get to your photographs so you can start reminiscing about those happy times and the sad times that can possibly turn into happy times. Cherish life and the moments that are gladly given to us by our Lord Jesus Christ.

If you have a picture box, drawer, or hope chest full of old photographs then you are rich! Enjoy your wealth and share it with family and friends.

Yellow Squash Casserole by Tommy Cross

5 – 7 squash, cleaned and chopped
1 medium onion, chopped
½ cup butter
2 cups shredded cheese
1 Tablespoon sugar
8 – 12 ounces Italian bread crumbs

Boil squash and onion with the sugar until tender. Drain and stir in butter and cheese. Pour into an 8" or 9" baking dish and cover with Italian bread crumbs. Bake at 350 degrees for about 30 minutes or until top is browned.

I have served this side dish several times in my Tea House. Easy to prepare and all the ladies enjoy.

3 cups white cornmeal (not self rising)

2 teaspoon salt

1 ½ teaspoons baking powder

¼ cup milk

1½ cups water

⅓ cup butter

Grease a baking sheet and set aside.

In a large bowl combine the cornmeal, salt and baking powder. Moisten with milk. Add the water to make the batter smooth. Let the batter stand for 8 minutes. Add the melted butter.

Shape the batter into small patties about 4 inches long. Place the patties on the prepared baking sheet. Bake at 425 degrees for 20 minutes. Serve warm. Makes 18.

Elvis Presley became a famous singer and entertainer in the 1950's. He was a country boy who loved country food. Corn Pone is a form of cornbread he enjoyed but we always call it cornbread.

I remember the first time I heard Elvis on the radio. I ran about three blocks to see Charlotte, my friend. Her family owned the local dry cleaners and the family lived in the back part of the building. She was so excited because she and two of our other friends, Shelby Jean and Jeanie Lynn, had been to Memphis and stood in front of Elvis's home. They brought dirt and rocks from his front yard! My daddy bought the Elvis record for me so I could play it on my record player for everyone to enjoy. My friends and I learned all the Elvis songs and enjoyed many hours singing and dancing away the summer days.

The picture is my Brother-in-Law, Joe. Yes, he loves Elvis Presley!

For our Mother's 85th birthday, Joe and Sherry sponsored a Birthday bash complete with talent contest. Of course Joe "Elvis" won the prize!

So many things are taken for granted. How often we hear this spoken but at some point in our life we all experience loss of some kind and often many, many losses.

On February 2, 2018, at 4:30 PM, a house burned down. Not just any house, my sister Carolyn and Bob's home was destroyed by a fireplace malfunction. Carolyn discovered the flames billowing out the French doors on the second floor in the additional master suite. She called 911 and they jumped into action to save themselves, their pets, Spot and Tiger, and two of their three vehicles. The firefighters arrived in eight minutes and squelched the flames after some time. The Home burned so rapidly that there was little left to save. What was not burned was declared unsalvageable because of water and smoke damage. A beautiful three-story brick and stone home with a lake view along with a house full of antiques, family pictures and beautiful memories were snatched away in an instant. The most important miracle was the saving of lives.

Carolyn and Bob are members of a First Baptist Church in their little town. They are forever talking about their wonderful church and the friends that are like family. The most heartwarming thing happened. Those church members started coming from everywhere. Some brought food and drink, some brought warm coats and clothing and everybody brought love. Kim, their next door neighbor, was there offering storage in her garage for the few items they retrieved and anything else she could help with. Some of the friends offered housing to Bob and Carolyn. Eddie and I were there the next day after the fire and there was my sweet little sister Carolyn standing in front of her burned down home with that signature little smile of hers. I started crying but I was so relieved to just see her.

We met two more amazing people, Steve and Mary Nell. Mary Nell and I walked the two dogs, Tiger and Spot, and I came face to face with a woman that truly loves the Lord. It was uplifting to listen to her share some of her life stories with me. Steve and Mary Nell insisted that Bob and Carolyn share their home with them until temporary housing could be arranged. I knew my sister was in good hands and Eddie and I left with a peace of mind that all would be well. At that point no one knew how long it would be but that was not important. Do you know Bob and Carolyn lived with Steve and Mary Nell over five weeks! Can you imagine having anyone staying in your home for five weeks with two dogs, a pit bull and a dachshund, and never complain!! Carolyn said it was like a vacation. Mary Nell cooked everything, did everything, and everything and everything. ☺ Bob and Carolyn have always loved them but now they are like sisters and brothers. Can you believe this? The day Carolyn and Bob were scheduled to move Steve asked them, "Would ya'll stay one more night?" They stayed one more night! Hallelujah, Praise the Lord, what friends! The next day they moved into a little three-bedroom, two-bath furnished home that other friends owned. They will be rebuilding on their beautiful lot by the lake.

So many people have done and are doing so much for my family. The outreach demonstrated in the little town and the First Baptist Church are what living and loving the Lord is all about.

Thank you Jesus for all the loving kindness, I know I and my family have been blessed immeasurably.

"O Lord Almighty, blessed is the one who trusts in you."

Psalm 84:12

This is the house that burned.

How big is your world? How expansive are your windows in your world? Windows and worlds come in all shapes and sizes. I decided many years ago that I was going for the biggest and the best in my world and windows. Life decisions start from within and you can guide and control your threads of life to develop a future you can only imagine. The door is open — come on in!

The reference to windows usually conjures up thoughts of windows installed in homes, vehicles, or anywhere you need light. For several years I always had this dream home I wanted to build with gigantic windows in the living room. In 1970 my dream came true. We purchased four acres of farm land in the Arkansas country which proved to be perfect for my home with the eighteen-foot windows in the living room. The big outside world filled the room with a vast array of happiness and happenings. I hardly ever closed the curtains. My baby girl, Carol Ann, was born in 1971 and we enjoyed just sitting on the living room floor and looking at the big outside world. The twenty-foot Christmas tree lighting and adorning was a family affair. The beautiful treasure in the open window was enjoyed and shared with many friends and neighbors. Each year in the summer and fall a huge cotton field was located across the road in front of our house. I could observe the cotton choppers and cotton pickers removing the weeds with hoes or pulling a cotton sack while picking the cotton by hand. I knew it was hard work because I did this with my mother when I was a young girl. I sometimes baked cookies or delivered water to these workers at the end of the cotton row. They were always friendly and appreciative. Their days were long because they traveled at least a hundred miles every day on a bus from Memphis to make a living in these fields.

In December 1978 we moved to LaGrange, Tennessee. We purchased an "A" Frame home with one acre of land. Windows were everywhere! The ceiling in the main area of the house was thirty feet and the room size was 30' x 40' with a 6'x 6' fireplace. Yes, the twenty-foot Christmas tree set very nicely in front of these windows. The upstairs consisted of one bedroom and bath and huge windows that opened onto a generously sized deck. From the deck the view was trees, deer, and walking trails that could take you to infinity. Without hesitation the master bedroom was now upstairs and the deck was shared with family.

Our home now is sitting on a fifty-acre farm beside the Stones River in Tennessee. Our ranch-style brick home was built in 1985. The master bedroom has the most phenomenal windows! Curtain opening of a twelve-foot window reveals a panoramic view of Godly blessings and wonders that give an instant peaceful feeling. Beautiful sky, sunshine, trees, green pasture, deer, the wedding tree and a seventy-five-year-old barn are just a few of the adornments. Lying in bed and experiencing a rain or snow storm from this window is such a wonder. A second window overlooking the front yard is eight feet wide, where a view of the front yard reveals Martha's Tea House and a view of the Stones River.

I love my home, come and see more. Your windows and your world start with your heart. The Lord opens the door for peace and happiness. Have you searched for your Godly gifts?

"I am sheltered & protected in God."

Colossians 3:3

Early in life I realized I was different from the other children I played with in my hometown neighborhood. I was the only girl on the football team, I won all the talent shows in the neighborhood with my singing, and I never lost a card game on those long, hot, and lazy summer afternoons. Yes, everybody wanted to be my friend and I enjoyed the friendships and attention.

My Dad had high expectations for me and I felt like I was the most favorite little girl in the whole world. With his encouragement and praise I knew I wanted to experience life in a way my family could only dream about. Exploring venturesome territories and taking those chances that no one else dared to attempt were just the beginning of my life dreams.

I wanted to be an Eagle, free to fly the heights of Heaven, glide like an airplane and soar to the highest mountain tops in this big beautiful world. Yes, I was different but I realized I was part of a major network called family, friends, and life. I felt that my determination for success had to be strong and enduring enough so failure could never overtake my life dreams.

"Success is just a word unless you strive to make and keep it a part of your life." I was twenty-one years old when I graduated from public high school. Look in my high school annual and you will see this statement underneath my graduation picture. I like to think that I have always worked toward success but, just like you, I've had many challenges. Some you win, some you lose; but failures, disappointments, and challenges make us stronger. The stormy, challenging times come but you have to stay strong and courageous and know the Lord will bring you through and into the sunlight again. Never give up!

The world of working started for me at age twelve when I started babysitting. I added a few jobs along the way but for the most part I was in the medical field ten years and then a Real Estate Broker for thirty-two years. After retiring my real estate license at age sixty-eight I returned to writing short stories and poetry and opened a Tea House in Murfreesboro. I enjoy painting furniture, decorating, and baking. Bible Study and Book Club friends are important parts of my life. Everyone needs exercise; I choose to be a part of a Zumba dance class.

I am now seventy-four years old and feeling good about my accomplishments and life itself. Look around and see all the beautiful gifts we have every day. I don't separate success and failure anymore because they are just a part of this life and we are only passing through to better rewards.

The sunshine was beautiful today. I took a long walk and stopped to admire the deer in the backyard. I sang a song, watched the squirrels play, and baked muffins. Red birds were everywhere as I listened to their melody and wanted to fly away with them. After all, I am an Eagle—are you?

You know that special wish or dream that just keeps calling out to be fulfilled? We all experience these images, ideas, or emotions at some time in our life. If we are capable of such cogitations then surely our dreams or wishes can become reality at some level. I've had one such wish for many years and have even dreamed and made plans as to what I would do when the dream did become reality.

My Daddy died at the age of seventy-two in 1985 at home. I loved him so much. Through the years I have commented to friends and family that if I could only spend one more day with Daddy here on earth. So many things we could do. Not possible? Think again. Do you believe in miracles? Yes, I do, especially after the experience I recently encountered.

My dream came true. After many years of praying for this miracle the Lord granted eight hours for my Daddy and me to be together. I was instructed to drive to my sister Carolyn's home in West Memphis, Arkansas, at 8:35 AM. I did not understand why this location but my Mom and Dad always spent a lot of time with her family and I was sure this must be the meeting place for Daddy and me.

I rounded the corner off Rich Road onto North Roselawn, Carolyn's street, in West Memphis, Arkansas. There was my Daddy standing on her driveway! I had this feeling of being transported to a world that I had known as a little girl that only Daddy and I knew. He greeted me with his special little smile and a great big hug that only my Daddy could give. The summer day was bright, sunny, and perfect for our road trip down memory lane.

Daddy was dressed in his favorite overalls, short sleeve work shirt with pen in pocket, and his mechanic work boots. We had so much to talk about! I asked him about Heaven, he smiled and said just wait. I knew by the smile that he was happy and just waiting for all our family to be with him.

Daddy loved doughnuts so we visited his favorite place, Howard's Doughnuts, for a breakfast treat before we left West Memphis. We were in the car again and on our way to Joiner, Arkansas, our hometown. Upon arrival Daddy decided he needed a haircut so we stopped by his friend's barber shop, Joe Dean's, for a haircut and short visit. We were off again and crossed the railroad track in the middle of Joiner. I saw Daddy's face light up again. He saw "Hardhead" Edings standing in front of his Texaco Service Station. He could hardly wait to get out of the car and greet his best friend with a hearty handshake and bear hug. They could talk forever! When we left "Hardhead" gave Daddy a Texaco cap to wear for the rest of the day. Seemed like they had an understanding of what was happening.

We didn't have to go very far to see something so special to both of us, our home. Daddy and I held hands, walked upon the front porch, sit down in the old familiar swing and started swinging, just like we had never left. We walked through our home, room by room, stopping in the kitchen for Daddy to make a glass of iced tea for us. We talked about the Christmas trees we enjoyed through the years. Our stockings were always filled with fruit and candy and waiting for us to explore on Christmas morning along with all the presents.

Daddy's garage, "South's Garage," was next door to our home and was the next stop. He saw the tall bucket I stood upon as a child to help him take inventory once a year. We laughed about how we didn't know how to spell half the parts he had stored so we guessed. We knew what was there, even if no one else knew. We saw the battery chargers, jacks, and all sorts of tools. The big pot-belly stove stood in a corner where Daddy burned coal to keep warm in those cold winter days and sometimes nights.

Daddy's garden was located at the edge of a bean field on the other side of our home. We walked up and down the rows looking at the tomatoes, okra, peas, and pole beans. The pole beans were his favorite but the big ripe tomatoes were extra good because they had been grown by Daddy.

Granny and Pa Edings were sitting in their front yard across the street. We stopped and visited for a while. A slice of Granny's lemon meringue pie was most delightful. They were peeling peaches for canning so we peeled a few, gave them a hug, and continued on our special day.

We slowly drove around Joiner just looking at all the stores and shops. Akle's Grocery and Ice House, Faulk's Dry Goods, Wallace Miller Grocery, Bus Station, Chinaman's Grocery where we shopped each week, and Silverstein's Clothing were just a few that we had time to talk about.

We had to say hello to Mr. and Mrs. Allensworth who were stocking their fruit stand for Saturday shopping. Daddy had to have his favorite fruit, a banana, and I'm partial to apples.

Daddy wanted to see Harley and Nora Mae, Daddy's sister, who lived in the country across the levee. When we crossed the levee they saw us coming. They could not believe their eyes! They were shelling purple hull peas from their garden while sitting under a big oak tree. Daddy loved to shell peas so we grabbed a pan and helped them finish the bushel. When we finished the peas Aunt Nora Mae had a big country dinner for us. We ate while Aunt Nora Mae and Daddy laughed and talked about their childhood. As children it sounded like they got into a lot of mischief. After a little walk to the pasture to look at the cows, we said our goodbyes with big hugs and "I Love You" to both of them.

I just knew the next stop would really excite and please Daddy. We drove two miles to Bassett to visit Mother and Daddy's church, Bassett Church of God, which seated about fifty people. We walked into the church and Daddy felt right at home. He commented that he was dressed and ready to go to church on that Wednesday night when the Lord had other plans and took him to Heaven. He talked about it being such a glorious trip. There are no worries, no pain, just praising the Lord. We found a song book and sang "Old Rugged Cross" and "I'll Fly Away." We got on our knees and Daddy prayed a beautiful prayer asking for blessings for everyone. We thanked the Lord for this special day we were sharing. We left a gift at the pulpit, closed the church door, and left. We did not want to look back.

The special day was about to be gone but never forgotten. I drove and we talked all the way back to Carolyn's. He did tell me all our loved ones who are with him in Heaven said hello and they would see us in the by and by. The day was about gone but we were not sad. We were experiencing such a peace together. He knew I was still his little girl and I could tell he was anxious to go back to Heaven. The Lord was expecting new Christians that night and he wanted my Daddy to be there to meet them at Heaven's Gate.

I rounded the corner again on North Roselawn and Carolyn's house was in sight. We were truly happy! We hugged forever and prayed again, but no tears were shed. Such a blessing it was that day! I promised Daddy we would all see him in Heaven and he said "of course" and smiled. We looked at each other one more time, I closed my eyes and my Daddy was on his way back to Heaven—HOME.

Thank you Lord.

"Faith makes all things possible."

Matthew 17:20

Have you ever thought about becoming a medical doctor, attorney, teacher, decorator, banker, nurse, or a certified public accountant? If you are like most people you immediately think about time involvement and finances to accomplish one of these vocations. Why would you want to spend time and money becoming one of these people when you can obtain a real estate license and experience any or all of these professions! Well, not totally, but through a Buyer or Seller's eyes, they think you know it all and can do it all.

In 1979 I left the medical field to become a Real Estate Agent/Broker. I began my profession in Collierville, Tennessee, and ended it thirty-two years later in Murfreesboro, Tennessee. I became a life member of the Million Dollar Sales Club, Certified Residential Specialist, Certified Property Staging Consultant, Relocations Director, Managing Broker, and a Commercial Agent for development of Strip Shopping Centers in four states. There were many more awards, plaques and trophies which eventually ended up in the trash can. Plaques, trophies and awards are not what real estate is.

The Real Estate Profession is about helping people. Challenges come and you have to be ready to help at a moment's notice. Real Estate is not a "one size fits all." Strong commitment, knowledge, professionalism, and compassion are some of the strong qualities one must possess. People rely on their agent to guide them through the process of selling, purchasing, renting, or investing in a property. This process requires "many hats." Know the family/buyer/seller/agent, listen to their particular needs then diligently seek to accommodate those needs in a professional manner. Commission for the agent is not the main objective. If you treat people as you would like to be treated then the money will come and all will be well. The best feeling in the world is to know you have built trust with a seller or buyer. This process is called "REFERRALS." They will tell all their friends----always do your best!

I had so many wonderful, wild, sad and happy memorable moments as a Real Estate Broker. One of the most important things I learned is that a seller/buyer will tell you serious or personal matters that even a spouse does not know. That is strong trust, respect it always.

I have a degree in washing dishes, making beds, vacuuming, moving furniture, babysitting, painting, home staging, cooking, chauffeuring, counseling, referring, or recommending all kinds of services to homebuyers/sellers. Did I tell you I was a Real Estate Broker!! Doesn't matter, you do what you have to do to help build their confidence and trust in you. Sometimes it may mean washing a few dishes, dusting, rearranging furniture, or picking up clutter before a home showing. Your main objective is to properly show and sell that house. When you are selling, it's a house but when they are buying, it is a home. Bringing in a Professional Home Stager and/or Decorator may be necessary to help a seller understand the process of marketing and selling the house.

The life of a Real Estate Agent requires flexibility, but you know that, don't you! Out-of-Town Buyers are in for one day to purchase. Whoops! There goes dinner with the family tonight.

Just do your best, show respect and kindness and the Lord will do the rest. Being a Real Estate Broker for thirty-two years were some of the happiest and most fulfilling years of my life. I now spend time enjoying my Tea Room on our farm with all my friends and writing short stories and poetry.

Being a Real Estate Agent/Broker requires wearing many hats… And I was easy to recognize, because I always wore one!

May 8, 2017

Can you imagine working with happy people in a happy environment and every person that comes through the front door every day is also happy? Free travel to many parts of the world that you ordinarily would never see in your lifetime is included. You can actually enjoy getting out of bed and going to work to help people. Who are these happy people you have the privilege of helping each day? Enter the world of a professional Travel Agent working with a highly esteemed owner operated Travel Agency. Surprised? No world is perfect of course but working with this company was a college education in the world of travel for me.

I knew nothing about the travel industry but this company decided to take a chance on educating and training me to be one of their best travel agents specializing in cruises. I was so excited about this opportunity and the first thing I noticed was all the happy people who came in to inquire and plan their travel. They were ready to make plans for their long-awaited family dream vacation, a honeymoon, anniversary, or just some sort of getaway. Often times the entire family was there to help make decisions. The happiness was contagious in the office and everyone was personally welcomed.

The challenge was becoming familiar with the many cruise lines, ships, and the varied amenities. After several courses and at-home study I was ready to meet and greet these happy people and help to make dreams come true. Caribbean Islands and Alaskan cruises were favorites of mine. Although I had not yet traveled to any of these magical places, with the use of brochures and my cruise training, I became very successful in a short time.

My first trip was not a cruise. The Owner closed the travel agency on December 19th and we traveled to San Francisco for four days. Pier 47 is where we took residency for this exciting trip. We toured hotels, went shopping, and did some sightseeing. I was amazed at Union Square and the lovely grand hotels. I had never seen anything to compare to this. We wanted to shop at Neiman Marcus but the department store was at shopping capacity so we had to take a number and stand out front until some of the happy shoppers decided to leave. We crossed the Golden Gate Bridge, visited the giant redwoods, and traveled to Sausalito for more shopping and private dining on a luxury yacht in the San Francisco Bay area. This amazing trip helped me to build confidence in the world of travel and was a beginning to a new career.

My duties eventually expanded into planning Disney World, Disney Land, Grand Canyon, and Las Vegas vacations, just to name a few. The cruise travel was still my favorite with so many destinations on one cruise in one week. I traveled them all by studying brochures, booking the cruises, and never leaving my office for a few months! My first cruise was with Norwegian Cruise Line and St. Thomas was a favorite port of call. After that first cruise I wanted everybody in the family to experience this magic getaway with me. So many cruises were shared with family and friends.

The World of Travel was one of the best learning experiences I have ever encountered. I appreciated the opportunity, met interesting people, and found a happiness and satisfaction in my life that I had never known. Happiness is just a good feeling meant to be shared with everyone.

Penny's Chicken and Dumplings

To know Penny is to love her. She was raised in the cotton fields of Arkansas. I met Penny in a Zumba class at the YMCA in Murfreesboro and our friendship has grown through the years. Her business is called *Penny's Piddlin.* Arts and Crafts are her specialty. She makes beautiful custom shirts, Christmas ornaments, caps, scarves, pillows, and so much more! Penny created a keepsake dish garden for me depicting the resurrection of Jesus Christ and it stays on display in my tea house year round. Come to Martha's Tea House and see it. Lovely thoughtful gift, that's Penny!

BROTH FOR DUMPLINGS:

    8 cups water
    ½ stick butter, melted
    5 bouillon cubes
    7 uncooked chicken strips

Boil chicken with bouillon cubes until tender, remove from pot, cool and pull apart. Place chicken back into pot and add 1 can cream of chicken soup and the melted butter. Broth is ready for dumplings.

DUMPLINGS:

    2 cups all purpose flour
    ½ cup milk
    ½ cup water
    2 eggs

Mix these 4 ingredients, batter will become stiff. Divide into 3 parts.

Pour 2 cups flour and ⅓ dough mixture onto large work surface. Knead the dough and flour together enough to roll out, pizza thin. Cut into long strips then into shorter strips. Repeat this process until all dough is prepared. One at a time drop the dumplings into boiling chicken broth and turn down heat. Work rapidly using a large spoon to stir in the dumplings. Great family recipe.

Rossville, Tennessee 38066
February 9, 2016

Sometimes you never know where your ideas or dreams will lead you but you have to believe in yourself and act upon those dreams and ideas. The first step toward success was taken when you had these thoughts. Now it is totally up to you. You can dream for a lifetime, but action has to be taken to achieve goals in our lives. In July, 2002, it came time for me to act upon a dream that I wanted so badly I knew I had to find a way to make it come true. I bought my Mother a home!

I was the first to move from Arkansas to Tennessee. After a few years all the family members became Tennesseans. My Mother moved into a small apartment in Rossville, Tennessee. Being the sweet Mother she is, she became acquainted with everybody and made so many friends. One of these new friends decided to sell his house located on Second Street in the historic district of Rossville. Mother called me and I immediately bought it before the sign was in the yard! Gosh, what did I just do! This little two-bedroom, one-bath home was perfect for a perfect Mother. We painted, decorated and furnished it just the way she wanted it. Mother was so happy and enjoyed living there. She could walk to the post office, bank or the local restaurant in five minutes. The neighbors loved her and were sad to see her leave when she moved to my sister's home in Collierville.

Mother's home was located on a one-acre lot with the back part of the lot facing Third Street. I had the lot surveyed and discovered I could build another house facing Third Street. The only way I was allowed to build this home was to subdivide the lot. I had to obtain permission from the town council and meet all the building requirements. The town council declared that this property would have to be a new subdivision with a new name. I wanted to honor my Mother by naming it "Miss Mable's Gardens" but that name was not allowed. So the dream was finished when the council suggested "The Martha Lloyd Subdivision." Everyone liked and approved this idea and construction started on the four-bedroom, three-bath, 2600-square-feet home. Upon completion of my new home I gave an Open House inviting neighbors and town officials to come by for food and drinks. Over one hundred people visited my new home that day! I was so excited and amazed beyond belief! A beautiful home built by Buck Thomas, a builder I had represented for years. I think he was almost as proud of this accomplishment as I was.

I dreamed really big! It was small steps at first but all these small steps became so big that I could not stop. I knew it would happen if I prayed, worked smart, remained confident, and believed in myself. I wanted this dream to become reality because my Mother needed her own home. I was blessed beyond my dream. I presented the perfect home to my Mother and created a subdivision with my name on it: "The Martha Lloyd Subdivision"!

Life is such a gift and blessings are waiting for you. Your first battlefield is your mind. Remove the distractions and listen because God does care about the details of your life. Whether big or small just dream, pray, ask for guidance, and ACT!

Mable's new house.

A house from the Martha Lloyd subdivision.

The Rolling Store

October 1999

Hurry up Carolyn, put down your cotton sack,

The Rolling Store is coming, we will be right back.

Full of goodies and always on time,

We could get candy and soda pop for only a dime.

You have never heard of a Rolling Store?

Well, just listen and I'll tell you more.

A great big old bus full of ice cream, food, and drinks,

Just what you wanted to see coming down the gravel road to get your back out of the
cotton sack kink.

The Rolling Store was for people living in the country who had no transportation to
town,

Dry goods, brooms, mops, pots and pans, and groceries would abound.

It came down the country roads on a regular route,

If you needed something, the Rolling Store would have it without a doubt.

You could hear the horn blowing a mile down the road,

All the people would be waiting by the roadside to lighten his load.

The bus had to be stocked early AM.

It didn't return until the evening sun was very dim.

You step on the bus and just shop, shop, shop,

For one thin dime you could buy a candy bar and soda pop.

The Rolling Store demanded long hours and a lot of hard work,

There was never any theft and you didn't have to worry about being hurt.

The store could be orange, yellow, red, or green,

In the afternoon it was the most welcome sight we had ever seen!

The Rolling Store has been gone for many a year,
It is part of many memories I hold very dear.
I have often thought it would be nice to revive this store,
I know if I started one then the people would want a hundred more.

The Rolling Store helped many families to make a living,
Sore muscles, tired feet and aching backs, the big colorful bus was unforgiving.
The bus was a family's way of life,
Working together in harmony without a lot of strife.

Oh, Carolyn, if only we could experience the Rolling Store one more time,
Just think what we use to buy with our only thin dime!
I would have to have a soda pop, I am dying of thirst.
But, like a big sister should do, I will let you shop first.

So hurry up Carolyn and put down your cotton sack,
The Rolling Store is waiting, it is right on track.

2 cans of 8-count Crescent Rolls

¾ cup mayonnaise or salad dressing

½ cup sour cream

16 ounces cream cheese, soft not melted

1 envelope Ranch Style dressing mix

1 cup grated cheddar cheese

¾ cup each (or more): chopped---green pepper, green onion, broccoli, cauliflower, carrots

Just use your favorites for topping

Cover an 11 x 13" or 11 x 17" pan with crescent rolls. Pinch seams together. Bake at 350 degrees for 10 minutes or until lightly browned. Cool.

Mix the mayonnaise, sour cream, cream cheese, and dry dressing mix together and spread evenly over the roll crust. Prepare vegetables, toss together and sprinkle over the crust.

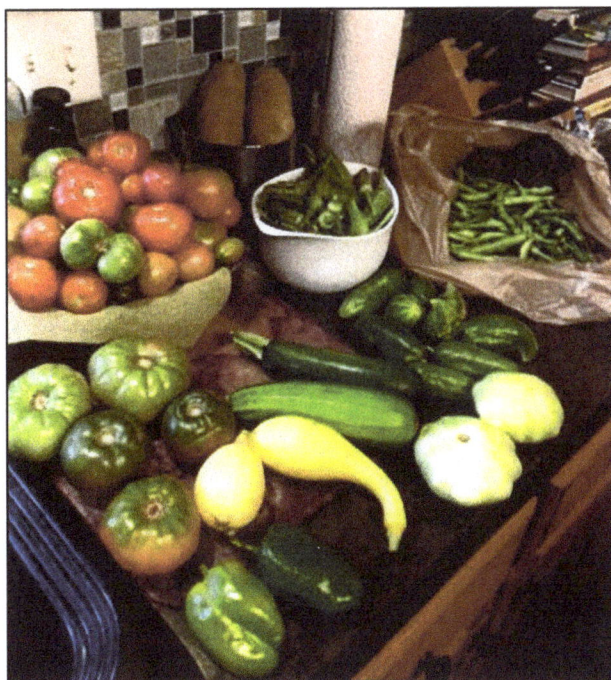

Vegetables from my
son-in-law's garden (Mark Cross).

Sprinkle with grated cheese. Cover with plastic wrap and press lightly to push vegetables down. Refrigerate 3 – 4 hours before serving. Cut into desired sized pieces and serve.

Can be made 1 day ahead of event and refrigerated. Makes a lot! Crowd Pleaser!

Allie, the loveliest of lovely friends, served this dish as an appetizer at her home in 1978. I'm sure through the years I have served it over a hundred times at my home, tea room and open house gatherings for homebuyers.

Our Beautiful Baby Doll

June 10, 1999

Born October 19, 1959 in the middle of the night,
None of our family ever dreamed she would be such a delight.
Mother Mable was forty and Daddy Johnnie was forty-eight.
The birth of this little angel was certainly late.

Mom and Dad allowed me to name her Sharon Lynn,
I knew she would go places a South had never been.
Sharon had jet black hair and bluest of eyes,
It was just impossible for me to ever tell her goodbye.

She went everywhere with me, holding her in my arms,
She was always noticed, she had such charm.
She was the talk of the town, that's not to be denied,
Sometimes she put Mother in such a state to be tied.

Sharon brings so much joy and pleasure, not to mention fun,
There is no one who does not love her, not even one.
She is a brave and young beautiful lass.
Sharon is my little sister with all the right class.

Today Sharon is a wife, mother, friend, and nurse,
All the scenes have been played, no need to rehearse.
She is genuine all the way to the core,
Sharon is my beautiful little sister, who could want more.

Our Beautiful Baby Doll is loved by all,
She has big brown eyes and a winning smile, standing only five feet tall.
Sharon is kind and considerate and has a great big heart,
I know God will protect her and we will never be apart.

My little sister, Sharon Lynn South,
Born October 19, 1959, she is a joyful bundle to shout about.

Mable's Magic

My Mother, Mable Corrine Sparks South,
Few People knew what she was all about.
Yet her life was an open book,
If you would only take the time to look.
I've seen her give to the poor as well as the rich,
She has pulled many people out of life's sometimes hopeless ditch.
If she had a dollar it was yours,
Yes, Mable Corrine South was a Doer.

My Mother Mable was loving, kind, and didn't mind hard work a bit,
If you ever thought you would get the best of her,
You may as well quit.
I've seen her pick cotton all day and cook all night,
But she always took time for her family, her life's delight.

"Maybelline" was the cutest little Mother I've ever seen,
She dressed every day like she had just stepped out of a fashion book,
If you ever saw her you had to have more than just one look.

Mother had a passion to always stop for garage sales,
Regardless of rain, snow, sleet, or hale.
She took great strides to save a dollar,
25-cent pants, 10-cent earrings, 50-cent shoes and pretty blouses—always with a collar.
Get out of her way, here she would come,
If you had bargains, she had to buy some!

Mother went through life putting herself last,
But she was one of the main players in life's great cast.
My Mother cared for her family as well as neighbors and friends.
Even when she was on her last leg,
This little Mother made it so you didn't have to stoop or beg.
Such a caring person was she,
Just half this good I would like to be.

Mother, you will never be gone, you are everywhere,
It's just that saying goodbye today is hard for us to bear.
You are a wonderful Mother and I can't pick up the phone and hear your sweet hello,
But I know you are smiling on each of us here below.

Go in peace and tell Daddy and Alvin Hi,
It is your children's mission to see the three of you in the by and by.

Mable Corrine Sparks South,
It's a privilege to say she was my Mother,
My mentor, my friend,
   and Rock of Gibraltar,
The things that life are all about.

Sleep well Dear Mother.

Do you know what it's like to live in a tent?
It cost $50.and was cheaper than rent.
Why would anyone live in a tent? Why? Why? Why?
At the time this is all Mable and Johnny could afford to buy.

I remember the tent, our home, remember it quite well,
Carrying water and building fires, freezing weather, it was a little bit of hell.
But after paying $200 for a lot in the city,
$50 is all that was left in the "kitty."
This way of living lasted about a year,
Trying to care for his family our Daddy always worked in high gear.

The time came when the tent had to come down,
A historical three-room home was the talk of the town.
The home had been a doctor's office which had to be moved three miles,
10' ceilings, giant bay windows, big front porch, our family was all smiles.
Daddy worked two jobs and Mother picked cotton,
All that hard work, a Mother and Daddy never to be forgotten.

We had a smokehouse, chicken house, and some great big pigs,
Our family grew to seven but never too big.
We were the first to have a refrigerator and TV,
Everybody came from miles all around to see.
Daddy bought a garage and was the best mechanic around,
If you wanted it fixed right, honesty would certainly abound.

In 1955 we moved just up the street,
A three-bedroom, one-bath home made the picture complete.
Indoor plumbing, ballroom size living room, swing on the front porch, and a crepe
    myrtle in the yard,
Times were so simple then, you didn't need a dog to guard.

Daddy's garage was located next door,

He spent twelve to fifteen hours a day walking and working on that concrete floor.

"Sister," he would say, "bring me some ice water, ice water," I'll never forget,

His special little pitcher, I still have it.

So many happy times and events,

To tell you about all of them I could hardly make a dent.

It was the home place with Queen Mable and Johnny as King,

My, what I would give to sit and talk with them just once more in that front porch swing.

Our loved ones pass on and time ticks away,

But the memories of our home and my dear sweet Mother and Daddy are in my heart to stay.

Birds are singing as I walk outside,
Dear Lord, thank you this day for being my guide.
Blue sky with white puffy clouds that remind me of cotton,
The days in the cotton fields with my Mother can never be forgotten.

Green trees, green grass, and colorful flowers abound,
The Stones River is just a breath away,
Listen for the gentle sweeping sound.

The turkeys have returned to the farm to explore and perch on the fence,
When they will leave again keeps us in suspense.

The deer are gathering in the pasture under the wedding tree,
They love to play "baseball" but today maybe there is a wedding, beats me!
These beautiful animals love to feast on my hostas and blooming flowers,
Midnight seems to be the magic feasting hour.

River Bend Farm is fifty acres surrounded by the Stones River on three sides,
When you go for a walk in the pasture or down the lane it seems like miles and miles.

Aunt Sarah Belle's Herefords, an English Cattle Breed, roamed and grazed here for
    years and years,
To see how much she loved them would often bring you to tears.
She cared for her cattle and worked full time at the VA,
When her little calves were sick she would surely miss that workday.
Her cattle were her pets and she gave them all names,
Without Aunt Sarah Belle Cooke River Bend farm will never be the same.

Oh my goodness! I could write all day about this "Little Piece of Heaven" that Eddie
    and I own,
We share our home and my Tea Room with family and many friends,
Once you visit you have to come back again and again.

"Do not be afraid or discouraged, for the Lord your God is with you WHEREVER YOU GO. "

Joshua 1:9

A Queen and a Princess in the Canine World,
Queen Laverne was yellow, Princess Shirley was black, two beautiful girls
Although they were sisters they were as different as daylight and dark
Everything they did just warmed your heart.

Born in September 1999, how cute these lab puppies were!
Carol went for one puppy but two became hers,
The black and yellow puppies were six weeks old,
That's when their life story with Carol began to unfold.

Laverne always greeted you with a great big smile,
She loved to impress you by carrying a limb or big stick for a half mile,
Laverne was a gentle loving "human" pet
If Carol was sitting, at her feet is where Laverne sat.

What a bark this dog had,
You would think she was really bad,
Not Laverne, so sweet and kind
She was a protector, friend, and the rarest find.

Shirley, what a pretty little pup!
If you could not find her then you knew something was up
She liked relaxing by the fireplace taking a nap
Shirley was quiet and did not like sitting in anyone's lap,
She was happy and pleased when you rubbed her ears
There were times when Shirley and Laverne could bring you to tears.

December 2012, sweet Laverne passed on
But, oh my goodness, she will never be gone!
March 2013, Shirley followed Laverne to the playground in the sky
Carol loved them so much, it was so hard to say goodbye.

My Dad - My Friend

Written in memory of Alvin Ralph Lloyd,
Father of Carol Ann Lloyd and my husband 27 years
May 15, 1999

Alvin Ralph Lloyd is my Dad,
He taught me that no matter what the problem,
Don't think of it as bad.

He was a talented honest man,
This Dad of mine,
Yes, he was truly one of a kind.

I remember my first puppy he brought home in a box,
For some odd reason we named him "Rock."
Daddy played with the puppy as much as I did,
At heart he was just a big kid.

A tender, gentle heart and a winning smile,
That's what you always saw with this Dad of mine.
He was generous and kind and would do without,
I would always get what I wanted,
There was never any doubt.

In the evening he always read me a book,
He didn't care how tired he was or how long it took.

Yes, Daddy was honest, quiet and shy,
And there was one thing he would not do,
That was to tell a lie.

Daddy, you were always such a great strength to Mom and me,
Now I want to ask "How can this be?"
I know you are happier now,
Bit I wish you were here,
As I shed each one of these tears.

Sleep Dear Daddy,
As you have never experienced before,
One of these days I'll be knocking at your front door.

You were loved by all and things just can't be the same
You will be missed and remembered by all the Lloyd and South gang.
Alvin Ralph Lloyd, my Dad and my Friend,
To your precious spirit there will never be an end.

July 1999

Can you believe a couple being
married a million years and
never having a fight?
The finest two people you would
ever want to meet, who worked
so hard with all their might.
They had a house full of kids and a
pickup truck,
But if you thought you would see
them anywhere but Joiner,
Arkansas you were out of luck.

Harley was born with very little
eyesight so Nora Mae was his
eyes.
They tended cattle, chopped
cotton, and raised a big garden
all under an Arkansas sky.
Nora Mae and Harley worked
together side by side,
She never seemed to tire from
being his guide.

Harley attended college and always enjoyed a nice chat,
He could talk all day while sitting under a shade tree and petting one of their many cats.
When there was work to be done Harley was at the front of the line,
Harley and Nora Mae were truly one of a kind.

They lived across the levee in the back side of nowhere,
Raising their children and sharecropping with very few cares.
They loved to have company and they didn't venture out much,
When our family visited them you could count on beans and cornbread for lunch.

Nora Mae canned food from the garden, jars were everywhere!
Peas, beans, tomatoes, corn, whatever, she didn't care.
She worked hard, never complained, and always had a smile,
You could see clean washed clothes hanging on a clothesline for a country mile.

Harley and Nora Mae were a favorite uncle and aunt,
To find two finer people you just can't.
Nora Mae died of cancer after a short while,
Sherry and I visited her in her final days and we left with a great big smile.
She had blue eyes, brown hair, and was thought of as a plain Jane,
No matter how hard she worked the smile would always remain.

Harley, oh such a sweet man,
He and Nora Mae were so compatible, they walked hand in hand.
Harley lived quite reluctantly for several years after Nora Mae had passed on,
Two people we loved so much are now gone.

I miss crossing that levee and seeing their great big home,
Our loved ones die all around us, I sometimes feel so alone.
We don't appreciate our loved ones the way we should,
If I could only turn back the clock, if only I could.

5 large bananas

1 large box vanilla wafers

5 cups milk (I use 2% milk)

3 small boxes instant pudding (vanilla or banana or mix)

1 large tub Cool Whip

1 cup sour cream

Mix milk and pudding with whisk until blended, add sour cream and ½ container Cool Whip. Layer vanilla wafers, sliced bananas then the pudding mix, ending with pudding and top with other half of Cool Whip.

Who wants Banana Pudding? I do! I do! Carolyn prepares this delicious pudding almost every Sunday. She and her husband, Bob, live on a lake and her daughter and family drive seventy-five miles to attend church with them each week. After church services they all pile into the car to go have lunch at one of the local restaurants. After lunch it is time for this delectable dessert, Banana Pudding, while sitting on their deck watching the boats floating by on Pickwick Lake.

No, you don't have to look too far to find a story about our Mother, Mable Corrine Sparks South. Mother was one of the most beautiful, talented and determined ladies I have ever had the privilege of sharing life with. Generosity, kindness, and love could also be middle names for her.

Mother passed on March 18, 2016 after a bout with colon cancer. She would have been ninety-six years old on June 1, 2016. She loved her family which was her greatest enjoyment in life.

I remember and shared so many lovely times with my Mother that I feel like I need to share some of those moments with our family. Those times were only moments and my heart is crammed packed with so much love and joy from these experiences.

These will be short, short stories in no particular order. I think about her every day and sometimes I cry and sometimes I laugh with those thoughts but I always receive a blessing because she gave so much to so many people and I was lucky enough to be able to claim her as my MOTHER. To know her was to love her, Mable Corrine Sparks South.

My hopes and prayers are to convey these life happenings in a way that would be a blessing, moment of happiness or a realization of life itself for the reader.

I'm excited! Thank you for taking your few moments to share a story or two about my Mother. Hopefully you will come away with an extra smile and more appreciation of your family. There is only one life on earth, no rehearsals. We need to get it right the first time so we can spend eternal life with our Heavenly Father. You don't have to be perfect, just forgiven.

Mable and the University of Memphis mascot.

The One Arm Bandit (for real!)

Seven o'clock in the morning and I'm on the phone with Mother. She is trying to decide where she wants to go for the day. After several minutes she blurts out, "I want to go to Tunica, Mississippi, to the casinos and gamble." I was silent for a minute and shocked! My Mother had never gambled like this in her life! What could I say? This decision was not open for discussion; her mind was set on having this experience in her book of life. So, to Tunica we did go!

We arrived in Tunica and, since I was not a gambler either, I knew very little about where to go. With casinos everywhere I just picked one, the Gold Strike (sounds pretty good, doesn't it?). We went in and I seated Mother in front of a one arm bandit, gave her $20 in quarters, and showed her (Ha!) how to conquer the bandit. I watched her a few minutes and she seemed to get the idea. I was looking at some of the other machines when I heard bells going off and lights blinking. I saw this expression on my Mother's face and it was her one arm bandit machine making her happy. Mother had won $50!! After gathering up her winnings she tucked her purse under her arm and said, "Let's go." Of course I asked why she wanted to leave after only twenty minutes. She informed me that the money was hers and nobody was getting the chance to take it away from her. She did not even want to stay at the Gold Strike Casino for lunch!

We always took time for lunch on these outings and she always chose the eating establishment. She liked Captain D's, Shoney's or just a hamburger satisfied her. Before we would finish the meal she was always, always reaching in her purse for money to pay the bill, which I refused. But this casino day was one day that nobody was getting my Mother's money.

I didn't tell a lot of people about this experience because there weren't any gamblers in our family that I knew about, and I didn't know how it would be received. A hilarious, fun, and exciting memory was created with my Mother that casino day.

I thought I knew most everything about my Mother but time is proving me wrong. She was always a surprise so there was no way you could imagine what she would do next. Since her passing on March 18, 2016, not a day goes by that I don't think of some little something that sparks a special memory. I think of these special memories because I loved her so much. Mother was always being creative with at least ten projects happening at one time. Mother Mable had such a "freshness" about her, whether dressing for the day or catering to her family and home. When my Mother arose in the morning she always dressed for the day and a housecoat or robe was never a part of her attire.

One project she did during the winter months was quilting. As children we hated it. The living room, kitchen, and bathroom were the only rooms in the house that were heated. Yes, the living room was the center of quilting for Mother and sometimes Granny Edings who would come from across the street to help. They both loved quilting. The wooden quilting frames were assembled in the living room. The fabric was secured to the frame and placed on five-foot-long wooden saw horses located at each end of the room. With the quilting apparatus in place there was very little room left to sit and watch television and only a pathway to the kitchen and bathroom. As Mother and Granny Edings quilted, laughed, and talked, the new quilt was taking shape one stitch at a time. This slow process could take a few days depending on how much fun the ladies were having and how many things they had to talk about. When the quilt was finished, the bulky, overpowering equipment was removed so a happy normal life could resume in front of the television. The patterns for the quilts included Dutch Dolls, wedding ring, flowers, and large brightly-colored squares of material that Mother had gathered from making clothes for the family. Today these quilts are prized possessions to soon be distributed to our grandchildren.

I remember one year when Mother was convinced that she could be the short order cook for the night shift at our local family restaurant. After 8 PM it was mostly heavy truck traffic that came through Joiner, Arkansas, our home town, traveling to Memphis and beyond. Mother worked 8:00 PM to 4:00 AM and Hazel Elrod, our next door neighbor, was the only night waitress. Mother could not read or write so Hazel wrote the customer order then read it to Mother so she could prepare the food. They were a team that made it work! Mother would arrive home about 4:30 AM and start making biscuits, chocolate gravy, and eggs for the family. Daddy ate and was out the door to make a living in his garage located next to our house. We were awakened at 6:00 AM to dress, eat, and then pile into the car so Mother could get us to school by 7:00 AM. Sometimes Mother would bring home a strawberry jelly roll cake or a chocolate cream filled cake that was delivered in the early morning to the restaurant. These delectable treats were enjoyed at night only after supper was finished and dishes cleaned.

Work, Work, Work was a big part of our everyday lives. We all worked together in harmony for the family. I am so proud of our Mother and Daddy. We were rich and did not know it! Love and Happiness are right under our nose every day.

Stop! Look! Listen! You can experience real life events you never know you have! Don't wait!

Mable

Written by Martha Lloyd Cooke:
a letter from her Daddy, Johnnie, to her Mother, Mable, March 12, 2016

My Queen, I have always loved you. I have been waiting for you. The Lord told me last night that He is preparing a special place next to me for you. You will arrive in Heaven any day now. I have joyfully gathered all the family to greet you when you arrive. Mable, you will be so happy here. I have talked to your Mother, Ada, and since you did not get to say goodbye to her when she left so suddenly, she wants to be the first to fold you into her arms and say welcome Home, dear daughter.

We have so many family members here in Heaven and all of them are excited about your arrival. I see my Mother and Father, Will and Rose South, every day and we get together with my brothers and sisters: Percy, Clifton, Gilbert, Russell, Jesse and sweet Nora Mae, Ludani and Alice. You remember that Ludani had only one leg and Alice had only one arm? Not in Heaven, every soul is perfect. So you don't worry about anything or anybody because God has this "dying thing" in his hands. Your life will just begin when you enter Heaven's Golden Gates.

I think about the first day I met you when you lived on top of that mountain in Alabama. I thought you were the most beautiful girl in the world and I waited two weeks to get permission from your Dad to ask for a date. You were so shy and quiet but I knew you liked me too. After dating for about six months I knew I had to have you as my wife. Your Dad said yes and you said yes. We didn't have any place to live so we traveled around living with my relatives until we could do better. We finally built a tiny house at the foot of a mountain with some rough lumber someone gave to us. I became a "shade tree" mechanic. We lived there until Daddy and Mama decided to move to Arkansas to pick cotton. We just loaded up and went to Arkansas with them. We share-cropped and picked so much cotton! We knew there had to be a better life so with your persistence we gave up sharecropping and moved to the closest little town, Joiner. I started the mechanic work again, you continued to pick cotton and we knew there was a future for us in Arkansas. I give you the credit for so many of our successes because I could be very stubborn sometimes and you would just take over decision making. We were blessed with a home and four beautiful, healthy children. At the end of their earthly journey we will be together forever here in Heaven.

81

Mable, wait until you see Ashley, Robert and Pam's little baby girl who lived only a few short days; she is so adorable. Ashley is one of the favorites and she and her sister, Haley Renee, play together every day. All children are special and perfect and greatly honored in Heaven.

Bertha, Needie Ailene, and Hubert, your two sisters and brother and Acel, your earthly father will be standing in line to welcome you. The perfect reunion will be so great. Especially with Needie Ailene who became a member of our family when she was six years old. She talks about all the cakes you made for Christmas and how you and I cared for her.

There are so many friends and family here in Heaven. I pray that one day not only our earthly family will be reunited in Heaven but that all earthly people will recognize and honor the Glory of God. I have to go for now but we will all be standing with the Lord when you arrive. What a glorious journey you are on!

January 13, 2018

"Perhaps they are not stars in the sky, but rather openings where our Loved Ones shine down to let us know they are happy." I recently read this expression in a book I was reading. Millions of stars in the sky and one of them is my Mother.

I have been trying to talk to her for several days but I know she is always looking for a new adventure in heaven. Yesterday I heard from her. I was telling her about how much I enjoy our Lunch Buddy program that I participate in through our church, New Vision Baptist Church in Murfreesboro, Tennessee. Mentioning lunch with children was all it took for her.

My Mother is amazing! She has been in Heaven for almost two years and during this time the Lord has blessed her with a special talent of helping to entertain and teach adults as well as children. Tea parties for all her friends are a specialty. But today she questioned me more about our Lunch Buddy program and the little girls and their families from whom I have received blessings.

Mother wants to start a Lunch Buddy program for all the little angels in heaven! So many little angels and they love to be entertained. She has a song that I taught her and she is going to teach the little angels this special song. She asked the Lord for extra help so all of them could learn the words to the song at the same time. Mother sang the song for me.

"I washed my hands this morning so very clean and white,
I lift them up to Jesus, to work for Him 'til night.
Little feet be careful where you take me to,
Anything for Jesus only let me do."

She thinks I should teach this little song to my Lunch Buddies. ☺☺ Great idea, don't you think? Mother had new little angels waiting and she was anxious to get started on this new venture. She promised to talk to me in a few days about her Lunch Buddy program and the "Little Angel Choir."

(The song was given to me by Aunt Alberta Sparks, Fort Meade, Florida. She is eighty-four years old and her Mother sang this song for her as a little girl and she has never forgotten it.)

This reminds me of my Mother singing in the cotton fields while we were picking cotton in the fields of Arkansas—what a treasured memory. ☺

Seeing the cotton fields while traveling on the back roads of Arkansas
always prompts me to stop and pick a handful of the white fluffy balls.

June 1, 2018

Yes, I heard from my Mother today. She has been in Heaven since March 18, 2016 and her feet have not hit the ground. But, I don't guess they have to with the big beautiful wings the Lord has given her. With the ladies' tea parties, children's choir, lunch buddies, new angels greeter and, and, who knows what else, she loves her new home. Today, June 1, 2018, Mother is ninety-eight years old and she had to tell me all about her birthday bash at 2:00 Heaven time.

Mother has no idea how many angels will attend so she decided the little angels could serve cupcakes and other refreshments from a lemonade stand. The little angels were excited about being a part of this happy event. Gallons and gallons of lemonade and all flavors of cupcakes were prepared and distributed to lemonade stands for everyone to enjoy. "Ring Around the Roses" and "Hide and Go Seek" were the two games the children wanted to play and I'm sure Mother will be right in the middle of these activities since they were two of her childhood favorites. Heaven is perfect and the party is about to start under the wedding tree out by the barn. Angels are fluttering in from all directions! Mother is visiting with a few angels she hasn't seen for a long time. There's our Daddy, John Henry South, and our Granny Edings! Daddy stays busy teaching little boy angels how to whittle and to whistle while they have fun. Granny Edings was always such a blessing to our neighborhood. She was everybody's granny. I loved walking to church with her on Sunday mornings. She helps to care for the new baby angels upon their arrival into Heaven. Mother is overjoyed with all the festivities. She has a surprise for everyone. Mother has taught the little angel choir a new song and they will be singing it for everyone to enjoy. With a big smile and clapping of hands the singing starts and their angel wings start fluttering as they sing "I'll Fly Away." (Mother and Daddy loved this song and I often sing it today when I think about them.) The ninety-eighth Happy Birthday song concluded and it was lemonade and cupcake time! Heaven is such a busy place but the angels always make time for special events, especially for my Mother.

I write this story to honor my Mother who loved life and family celebrations. She would have loved this special moment in our family. My daughter, Carol Ann Lloyd, was married to Mark Cross on May 26, 2018, in a beautiful rooftop wedding downtown Memphis. The Old Dominick Distillery was the setting with a view of the Mississippi

River, Arkansas-Tennessee Bridge, and the Pyramid. I tell you this about the wedding because as I sit watching the ceremony with vows being exchanged on that rooftop I felt a hand on my shoulder. Looking around I saw no one close to me. While sharing some of the wedding details with Mother I mentioned the "tap" on the shoulder. She told me it was her. She wanted me to know that all was well and Carol was beautiful and happy.

Do you believe in Angels? They are everywhere, readily available to give a helping hand. I'm sitting in a rocking chair under the wedding tree out by the barn just listening to God's world talking to me. You can hear the rapture, just listen. Maybe an angel will "tap" you on the shoulder.

"You can talk to God ANY TIME because He is listening ALL THE TIME."

"Call upon me and pray to me and I will hear you."

Jeremiah 29:12

At some point in our life there comes a time we must let go. "LETTING GO" is not easy and we never want to listen to people who tell us to listen and let go. "Who do they think they are, they don't know what I am thinking or feeling."

As I sit here on the sofa in my home with my favorite warm blanket and a soothing cup of fresh-brewed tea, I reflect on many secret feelings I have shared with this well-worn familiar covering as I gaze into the bottom of the tea cup. Thinking, praying for answers, reminiscing, singing a favorite song or enjoying the quietness are all a part of my visit with this special moment in time.

March 21, 2017, is a challenging day with this heavy heart, holding onto my security blanket, and gulping down the second cup of tea. March 18, 2017, marked one year in Heaven for my Mother and March 21 is the day she was buried in a beautiful pink casket which she had chosen. My thoughts about her wander from the happy times to the sad times and everything else in between.

I remember as a little girl how my Mother loved to sew. There was no money for fabric so she would sew dresses made from colorful flour sacks for Carolyn and me. She made us so happy and we looked so cute in our flour sack dresses when we attended school. I remember one that was green and yellow on a white background and I wore it for Easter. We never knew what the dresses would look like because she never had a pattern to follow.

Mother painted our home light pink one summer when I was about twelve years old. When she set her mind to something there was no turning back. Daddy just shook his head and let her go. Our home was a lovely light pink for many years and we all enjoyed it.

Two weeks before Christmas Mother started baking homemade cakes. She would bake for each one of us our favorite cake from scratch. With fifteen cakes in the house you could find about any flavor cake that someone would like, including the neighbors. She loved Christmas and she loved baking and cooking, no matter how many people she had in the house, which was never less than eight; the more the merrier.

Something she hated but she did it for her children: She picked cotton ten to twelve hours a day then come home and make supper for her family. The hard-earned money Mother made picking cotton was used for our school clothes and shoes.

In later years my Mother and I spent so many pleasant hours and days together. She could not read or write, other than her name, but we would go out for lunch and she would look at the menu, ask questions, place her order, and no one ever knew she couldn't read.

She loved living in Arkansas but her home state was Alabama. She loved going back there. Moulton, Alabama, is only about two hours away so we would drive early in the morning. We always visited her Mother's grave site, checked on a few cousins, aunts, and uncles, then returned home early evening. She missed her Mama who died when Mother was twenty-one years old, so seeing her grave site was comforting to her for about three months, then we would visit again.

My Mother, Mable Corrine Sparks South was just a lovely lady who never met a stranger. She talked to everyone, sometimes too much about too many things! ☺ She sometimes accompanied me when I was showing houses as a Real Estate Broker. I would be in another room with one of the buyers, walk back where she was, and she would be showing the room and telling what such a good price the house was and they needed to purchase it, because it was such a good buy. ☺

I tell these little stories about my Mother because these are just a few of the ones that I have been thinking about on this sad day, March 21, 2017. Somehow sitting here all safe and secure in my cozy blanket and sipping a cup of hot tea helps me to find solace.

I'll be back again here on the sofa or some other chair or room in my home, with my blanket and tea. Her picture is everywhere and it makes me happy to know she is happy and with our Lord Jesus Christ.

Do you have a special blanket that is just yours? If you don't, then you are just missing out on some quality time with yourself and the Lord. Seems like such a little thing but I have reclaimed so many important memories while lounging with my personal blanket—and drinking my special cup(s) of tea.

We must trust, honor, and obey the Lord. Use your blanket as a blanket of faith. Do you have holes in your blanket of faith? We all do. Identify the holes. God wants to fill these missing pieces with Himself.

March 21, 2017, still missing my Mother this afternoon but so thankful for the happy thoughts today and the reassurance that God does hear us and cares. God is everywhere, with me and you, but sometimes we don't look or recognize it. –

Did I just hear a bird sing? Thank You Lord. ☺

A Piece of Comfort:

"May the God of Hope fill you with all joy and peace as you believe in Him so that you may overflow with hope by the power of the Holy Spirit."

Romans 15:13

2 pounds ground beef
2 medium onions, chopped
2 green bell peppers, chopped

Saute onions and bell pepper until tender. Brown ground beef and drain any liquid. Combine onions, peppers and ground beef. ADD:

2 large cans, 28 ounce size, peeled tomatoes
3 teaspoons salt or to taste
¼ teaspoon paprika
½ teaspoon cayenne pepper
6 whole cloves
2 bay leaves
2 to 4 Tablespoons chili powder

Mix and simmer for 2 hours, add water if needed. Add 2 cans kidney beans and continue simmering 30 more minutes. Experience and enjoy!

A recipe straight from Minnesota that is a favorite of the family. Fran is the Mother of Luree, a bookclub member of the "Not Your Ordinary Bookclub." Fran enjoyed reading, playing bridge, walking around the lake at her home, and was a lifelong learner. Winter was her favorite season. I'm sorry to say that Fran passed in 2011 and is terribly missed.

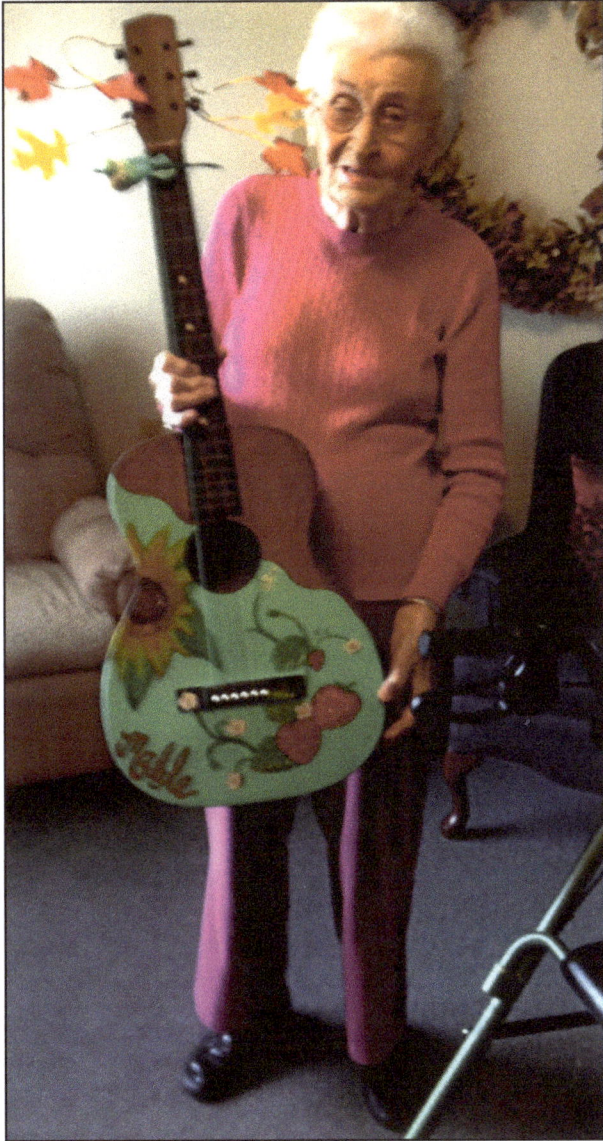

1942 finds my Mom and Dad sharecropping on a farm down by the levee about six miles from Joiner, Arkansas. They had moved from their home in the Moulton, Alabama, area to start a new life, sharecropping in Arkansas. No experience and no money soon presented some hard times. Did my Mother and Daddy quit? Absolutely not, no quitters here! My Mother conjured up a way to make a little money all in her own way. She had heard about a company that was offering an opportunity. If you could sell $5.00 worth of flower seed, you won a Gene Autry guitar, complete with his autograph! You guessed it! My Mother sold far beyond the $5.00 requirement for the guitar. Mother Mable received her Gene Autry Guitar!

You don't know who Gene Autry is? Mr. Autry was known as the singing cowboy. He was a favorite cowboy on television for over three decades beginning in the 1930's and was loved by all, especially my Mother. She would sing his songs and I can hear her now singing a favorite of mine, "Back in the Saddle Again." Carolyn, Wayne and I were in front of the television every week watching this cowboy. Gene Autry died in 1998.

This guitar has such a history! My Mother hung on to it through the years until 1959, when she gave it to me. My husband and I moved to Kansas City, Missouri, in 1961 and the guitar stayed with me. One day in the middle of the week when I was in school, my husband was home which was very much out of the ordinary for him. He had a surprise for me. He had sanded the finish from the Gene Autry guitar, including the special autograph and stained it a dark color! What could I do, the damage was done.

I have continued to cherish the guitar because it belonged to my Mother. It has traveled with me through twelve homes and three states. Four years ago Deneen Glidewell, a designer artist friend of mine, painted this special guitar. It is adorned with strawberries and sunflowers which were favorites of my Mother. The beautiful instrument is not playable but my Mom's name, Mable, is painted on one side and if I listen closely I can hear her singing "The Sweet By and By."

The guitar hangs in my dining room for all to see and most everyone asks about it when they visit my home. I proudly tell them the sweet story and I appreciate the smiles and caring. Mother has been gone since March 2016 but she knows I will never part with this priceless heirloom. My daughter, Carol, will be the next owner and I'm sure it will be on display in her home.

"Because our loved one is in Heaven, there's a little bit of Heaven in our home."

"God is our refuge and strength."

Psalm 46:1

Trail riders are coming down the turn road by the cotton field! Horses of all sizes being ridden by adults and children are prancing by. The monthly Marion, Arkansas, Saddle Club trail ride was being enjoyed by cowboys and their families of all sizes. Have you ever experienced horseback riding or just thought about it? A four-mile trail ride and stopping to have a picnic by a lake before returning home is one of the most exciting activities you can ever offer a child. Riding out through the country seeing the people picking cotton, watching for rabbits and everybody singing "Old McDonald Had a Farm" were just a few of the experiences we enjoyed.

Our trail ride started at the Griffin farm in Marion. Everyone met at the barn and helped each other prepare for this fun trip. Mr. Griffin had lots of gentle horses that he shared. Seeing all the children with their cowboy hats and toy guns was always special. One horse seemed to be the favorite so the cowboys and cowgirls tried to arrive early so Jim would be his/her horse for the day. Once we started on the trail it didn't really matter which horse anybody was riding. We were all like family because a big part of our lives were built around our children.

The Griffins were the most generous people in the world. They were always there to lend a hand to anybody that needed help. It was a Christmas tradition for Alvin, Carol, and me to go by and visit with the Griffins before traveling on to our families for the rest of

Christmas Day festivities. We had about thirty families in the saddle club and everyone loved the Griffins and the adventures that awaited them at their farm.

The Saddle Club had an arena where weekly horse shows were held every Friday night. What an event this was! Western Pleasure, Pony Under Harness, Walking Horses and Barrel Racing were just a few of the events. Everyone helped to care for the babies while one or both of the parents participated in their event. There was no charge to attend or enter an event but Mrs. Griffin was in charge of the concession stand so we always had great food and managed to have a little profit. The funds were used in December for a year-end party that was free to everyone. I was the Secretary and Treasurer for the saddle club for many years which required my presence at each meeting every month.

We always had a potluck dinner which meant that everyone liked to attend. There was a meeting scheduled for February 25, 1971, which I could not attend. The birth of my baby girl, Carol Ann, was happening! Once the saddle club found out that night they said "to heck" with the meeting and came to Crittenden Hospital in West Memphis to wait for the birth. They wanted to welcome our Carol Ann into this world. Such a joyous event and special friendship were bestowed upon our family that night. I couldn't believe the crowd! They had a party right there in the maternity waiting room and celebrated our Baby Carol's birth. Everybody had to see her before they left the hospital. For three days I had all our saddle club friends coming by to visit and bring flowers, candy and Shoney's Hot Fudge Cake. ☺

Now here we are forty-four years later and so many of these friends have passed on to a better place including my husband. I try to stay in touch with some of them. Those years were special and it was easier to have really good friends because families lived close. "It is not what's in the world but what is inside us that is important." Appreciate your loved ones!

1   pound ricotta cheese

2   cups shredded mozzarella cheese

1   egg

1   package frozen chopped spinach, thawed

1   teaspoon salt

1   teaspoon oregano

Dash pepper

32 ounces Spaghetti sauce (can be homemade—(I use Prego)

9 to 12 lasagna noodles, uncooked

In large bowl mix ricotta cheese, 1 cup mozzarella, egg, spinach, salt, oregano and pepper. In a greased 9 X 13 inch pan layer 1 cup sauce, 3 of the egg noodles and half of cheese mixture.

REPEAT. Top with remaining noodles and sauce. Sprinkle with remaining 1 cup mozzarella.

Pour 1 cup water around edges of pan. Cover tightly with foil and bake at 350 degrees for 1 hour and 15 minutes. Remove from oven and let stand 15 minutes before serving. Lasagna can also be assembled ahead of time and refrigerated until ready to bake.

This recipe was shared with me by my friend, Linda. I met Linda in 2004 when she came into my model home with a potential buyer. We immediately became friends. Sometimes friendships appear when we least expect them. Some are meant to be forever, like Linda.

Traveling the world can mean long exhausting trips, spending lots of money or seeking that one great moment somewhere out there that brings momentary happiness. While wandering around in places unknown one can miss the very happiness that is intended for mankind, LIFE. Nothing compares to holding and touching a newborn baby, counting the fingers and toes and hearing the first cry. You can hold that little precious baby so tight that you feel like your heart will just burst with joy.

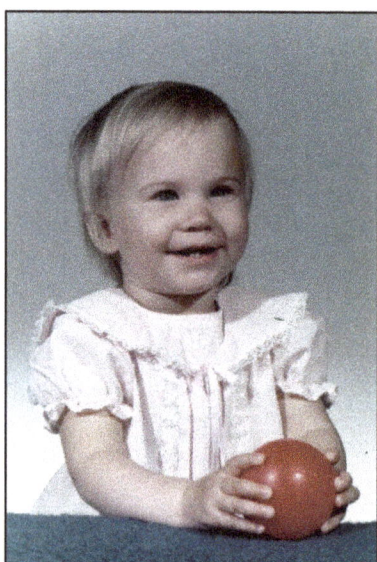

Carol Ann Lloyd was born on February 25, 1971 to Alvin R. and Martha M. Lloyd at Crittenden Memorial Hospital in West Memphis, Arkansas. Carol Ann weighed 6 pounds and was 19" long. Just a beautiful little girl with blue eyes and blond hair, I couldn't hold her enough! Four days later we took her home to our new home in the country. We didn't have many neighbors with children, so Carol played with her imaginary friend, "Locka." We lived in the country until Carol was five. During that time Carol had a pony named "Sugar" that she loved to ride. I would often find her at the barn sitting on her pony. She could climb up and into the feeding trough where "Sugar" was eating and then slide down her back. She would just be sitting there talking to her pony when I helped her to the ground. Her Dad would sometimes sit her in the saddle on his horse, "King," and lead her around and through the bean and cotton fields. Carol loved animals, especially dogs and cats. One afternoon her Dad came home with her first puppy and Carol named him Rock. This little puppy was a real companion and playmate to Carol for several years.

We moved to West Memphis for a few months before Alvin's company, Wedco, Inc., moved to Grand Junction, Tennessee. We bought a home a few miles away in LaGrange. Carol attended a private elementary school for two years. We moved to Collierville where she finished elementary and middle school. During these years she participated in dance and gymnastic classes. Carol started her "cheerleading career" with the elementary school flag football team in the third grade in Collierville. She cheered for Briarcrest Baptist School her four years of high school in Memphis.

Carol was a member of the Memphis State University Dance and Pom Pon Squad for four years. During this time they traveled to Spain, Italy, and Japan performing for the NBA McDonald's Classic. Travel also included trips to Chicago to perform at Chicago Bulls games and to Atlanta for the Atlanta Hawks games. The Memphis State University (University of Memphis) Dance and Pom Pon Squad have been National Champions for more than twenty years.

After graduating from the University of Memphis, Carol has continued her passion for coaching and choreographing. She worked with Frankie Conklin for seventeen years, teaching, coaching, and choreographing for many different high schools. Carol has coached and choreographed for the University of Memphis Dance and Pom Pon Squad for many years and the girls have taken the National Championship Award fourteen times under her leadership. She now also serves as the Spirit Coordinator for the University of Memphis.

There would be no way to list or try to tell anyone about the accomplishments Carol has attained in her life to this point. Her home office is filled with posters, pictures, plaques, trophies, and much, much more reflecting just a few of the life accomplishments. She has such a passion for life as well as her profession, her friends, her girls on the dance teams, her home and her dogs. Carol is so proud to be a part of the University of Memphis and to serve as Spirit Coordinator. She believes in doing the right thing and being fair with everyone. I have never known Carol to give anything less than a 100%. Her work ethics exude professionalism beyond anything I have ever experienced.

Carol and her two dogs, Sunny and Cher, live in her home that she had built by Buck Thomas a few years ago. The home sits on seven acres in Moscow, Tennessee. She opens her home many times during the year to out of town choreographers, coaches, her many friends, and professional "family."

What a Daughter! A Mother could not be any more proud than I am of Carol and the way she is living her life. Carol Ann is a beautiful lady both inside and out and will always be my best friend.

I Love You so Much and I am so happy and pleased that God gave me the best! ☺ Thank you Carol for your unconditional love for me!

May you always be blessed!

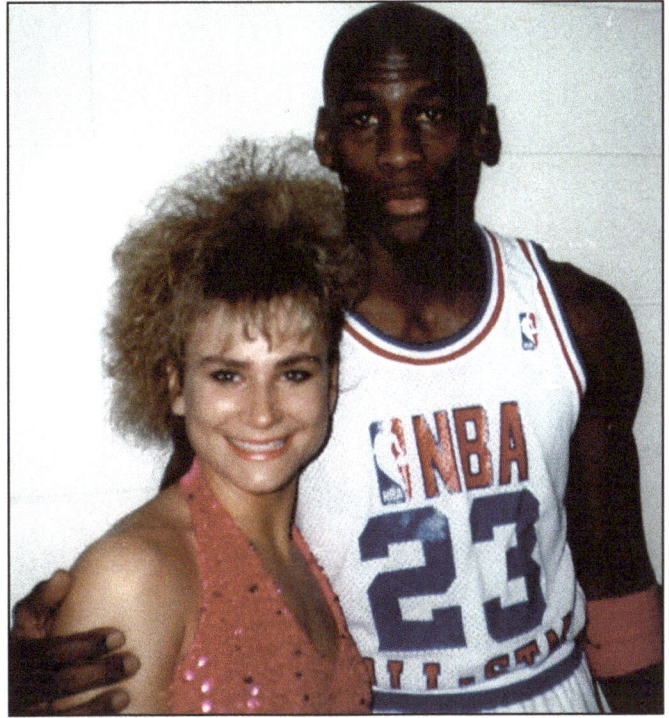

Carol with Michael Jordan (above), Bocephus (Hank Williams, Jr., left) and Magic Johnson (Carol is on the far left, below).

Carol Ann Lloyd and Mark Isaac Cross pledged forever love in a wedding ceremony on May 26, 2018, 7:00 PM, on the Rooftop of Old Dominick's Distillery located on Front Street, Memphis, Tennessee, with three-hundred-fifty guests in attendance.

The evening began with a Meet and Greet hour from 6:00 to 7:00 PM on the main floor with the serving of unique hordeuvres created by CFY Catering with a special "Crossopolitan" drink. Friends and family then gathered upstairs and outside on the rooftop. Carol arrived and was quickly ushered onto the elevator and upstairs by Ashley Oldham of 117 Events. Mark and Carol chose to not have bridesmaids or groomsmen. The wedding ceremony was officiated by Jereme Keith Smith, Pastor of New Life Church, Jackson, Tennessee, who is also Carol's first cousin.

The opening part of the "C C Rider" song by Elvis Presley prompted Mark and Jereme to enter and walk to the wedding stage. The musical lyrics of "Only Time" by Enya announced Carol's entrance to the wedding ceremony. She was dressed in a floor-length black wedding gown carrying her unique beautiful bouquet of red and deep purples with overflowing greenery. Eddie B. Cooke Jr., her stepfather, and her Mother, Martha Lloyd Cooke, escorted Carol to the wedding stage for the ceremony to commence. Carol and Mark were smiling, looking at each other, and feeling so comfortable in this beautiful environment with so many friends and family gathered just for them. Haley Smith, Jereme's wife, was in charge of the wedding bouquet while vows were being exchanged. Pastor Jereme prayed and the ceremony began.

The pledging of their love was beautiful. Mark placed the "Carol Custom Designed Ring" on her left hand and Carol demonstrated her love to Mark by placing a ring on his left hand. Jereme introduced Mr. and Mrs. Mark Isaac Cross to all attendees and the smiles were contagious with everyone cheering, dancing and cameras clicking. Joy in the house like I have never seen! Carol captured the most unique non-traditional fun loving Royal Wedding of Memphis, Tennessee. The special memories will live on!

The reception was 7:30 to 8:30 which gave enough time for guests to autograph a specially designed wooden board with Mark and Carol's photograph in the center. Three cakes plus special cookies, cupcakes, and more than enough food for everyone were on display. Special people who attended included Coach Carol's multi time National Champion Collierville Middle School and High School Cheerleaders and Dancers. The University of Memphis Cheerleaders and Dancers were on the scene with national championships that go way back to when Carol was a member of the dance team.

Couldn't be a party without these girls, they have all the "moves." Tim Bachus with Bachus Enterprises was THE Disc Jockey. He knew what these guests were looking for, especially when "Whomp, There it is" started playing when Carol and Mark entered the dance floor.

The beautiful wedding party ended at 11:00 PM and time had come for the Bride and Groom to depart. Everyone gathered downstairs on the main floor, waving the University of Memphis shaker poms and singing the fight song. Carol and Mark came through the crowd, entered the departing vehicle and waved goodbye. THE BEGINNING ☺

(FOOTNOTE) I met Mark on March 16, 2016 shortly after he and Carol started dating. They came to our house in Murfreesboro, Tennessee, and it didn't take long for me to like him. Mark was making omelets for everyone within a few hours and we barely knew him! That's Mark! I was also notified later in the day that my Mother had just died of colon cancer. What does Mark do? He gathered mine and Carol's hands and prayed for our family. Touched my heart—he was in. That's Mark. ☺ He also loves, loves his Mom and Dad and family. How can you go wrong with such a man! That's Mark!

Coconut Cream Cake

 1 box Duncan Hines Signature Coconut Supreme Cake Mix
 1 (3.4 oz) box coconut cream instant pudding and pie filling
 4 eggs
 1 cup water
 $^1/_3$ cup vegetable oil
 $^1/_3$ cup flaked coconut

FROSTING:

 1 can Duncan Hines Home Style classic vanilla frosting
 1$^1/_3$ cups flaked coconut

Combine cake mix, pudding mix, eggs, water and oil in large bowl. Beat at low speed with electric mixer until moistened. Beat at medium speed for 2 minutes. Stir in $^1/_3$ cup coconut (I use $^1/_2$ cup). Pour into pans or I use a 9 x 13, greased and floured or can use spray. Bake at 350 degrees for 32 to 37 minutes or when toothpick inserted in center comes out clean. Cool completely.

Combine frosting and coconut and spread on cooled cake. Sprinkle extra coconut on top if you like.

Refrigerate if not serving same day.

Enjoy!

Martha was the wife of Robert Jesse Cooke and the mother of six children: Robert L., Jesse, Sarah Belle, Eddie Buford, Kitty and Frances, who died as a little girl.

An awesome, beautiful lady who enjoyed gardening, Martha and Robert J. Cooke purchased River Bend Farm in 1896 and loved the farm. She never had any desire to leave it unattended.

"Martha" Mattie Cooke died in 1960.

7 oz. vermicelli, cooked according to package directions

1 medium onion, chopped

1 medium bell pepper, chopped

¼ cup margarine

¼ cup olive oil

4 oz. can mushrooms, chopped and drained

4 oz. can black olives, sliced and drained

16 oz. can tomatoes (I use the basil, garlic oregano style canned tomatoes)

1 cup shredded sharp cheddar cheese

10 ½ oz, can cream of mushroom soup

¼ cup water

Saute onion and bell pepper in margarine and olive oil until tender, add mushrooms, olives and tomatoes and simmer for 20 minutes.

Spread half of cooked vermicelli in bottom of 9 x 13 pan and cover with half of the sauce and 1/2 cup of the cheese. Repeat the layers again and top off with the cream of mushroom and ¼ cup water mixed. Bake at 325 degrees for 45 minutes.

**If you want meat in it, brown ½ pound ground beef, drain and add to sauce before you start layering in the 9 x 13 pan. I always double this recipe in a deeper pan because everyone likes it so well. Remember to double all ingredients.

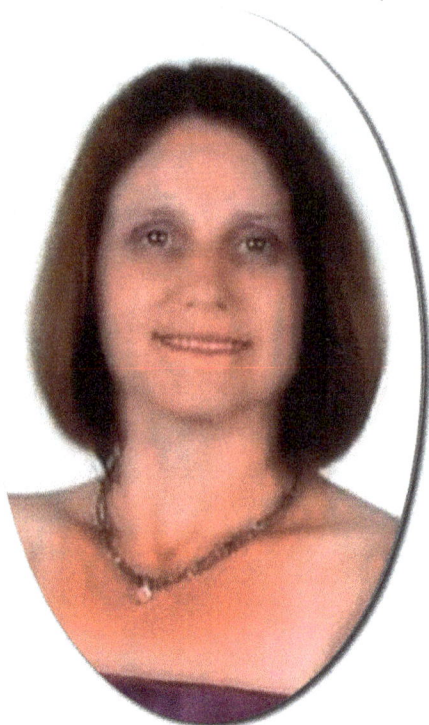

My little sister, Sherry, shared this recipe with me. She is an awesome nurse and worked many, many years in Memphis for one of the major hospitals. She has three granddaughters and spends much time entertaining them. One of her fellow workers shared this family favorite and it is always a crowd pleaser.

3 Tablespoons cocoa

3 Tablespoons self-rising flour

¾ cup sugar

2 cups milk

2 Tablespoons butter

1 teaspoon vanilla

Sift dry ingredients together, mix in milk slowly. Cook over medium heat, stirring constantly until thick and smooth. Add butter and vanilla. Serve with hot biscuits.

**We always enjoyed chocolate gravy because we always had homemade hot biscuits. Our friends wanted to spend many nights with us if we promised them chocolate gravy and hot biscuits for breakfast.

(Our Mother thought it was funny and she delighted in pleasing her children and their friends.)

2 3-ounce packages strawberry jello, dissolved in 1 ½ cups hot water
2 T. lemon juice
1   can whole cranberry sauce
1   small can crushed pineapple with juice
1 small can mandarin oranges, drained
½ cup chopped nuts

Mix all ingredients, pour into greased mold, chill.

September 17, 2019

3 or 4 family size teabags (as many as he wanted)
Sugar - probably a cup (whatever amount suited his taste)
Love - a whole gallon

Boil teabags, remove from heat, cover and steep for 2 minutes. Remove teabags, add sugar, stir. Say a prayer and place in refrigerator to chill. Gather the biggest ice tea glasses from the cabinet and invite your neighbors to come by and share a glass of Daddy's tasty tea, fun conversation and a gallon of love.

My Daddy was an overalls "kind of guy." He wore them every day except for Sunday church. The overalls attire was his uniform for most of his life. Daddy was a lifetime self-employed mechanic, other than the three years he and Mother sharecropped in the Arkansas fields, 1942 to 1946. In 1983 the family planned a trip to the beach in Pensacola, Florida. Daddy let us know he was not wearing short pants for this vacation. We didn't dispute him but we did purchase a pair of Bermuda shorts in hopes we could change his mind. One short walk on the beach and his mind had been changed! A bright sunny day, 93 degrees and the inviting water edge nudged him into the new Bermuda shorts! Once he wore the shorts there was no taking them away. He was so cute and lived in them at the beach. Daddy was "hooked" on his shorts and continued to wear them every spare moment he was not working on cars, trucks, tractors, buses, or anything else that had a motor. My wonderful happy Daddy, who everybody loved, passed in February 1985.

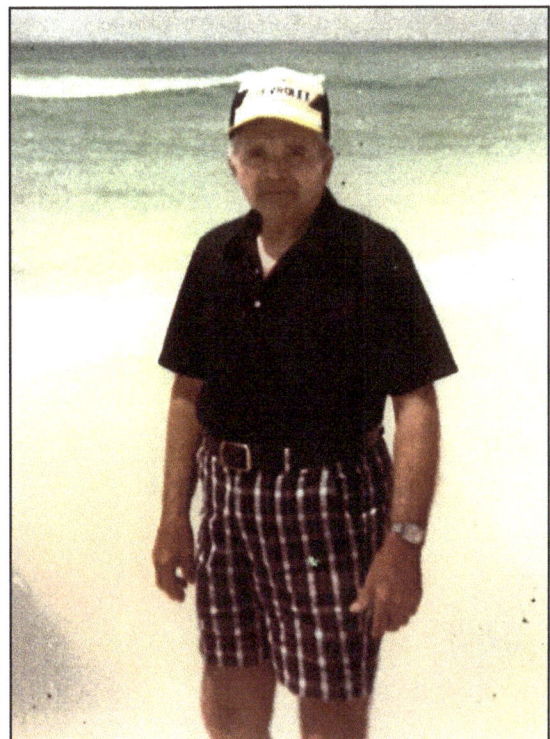

Because someone we love
is in HEAVEN,
Our HOME has a little bit of
HEAVEN

JOHN HENRY SOUTH

"Johnnie," Our Daddy

8—10 pork chops

½ cup fresh mushrooms sliced or 1 small can

Black pepper to taste

1½ cups water

Garlic salt

1 envelope dry onion soup mix

2 teaspoons vegetable oil

Sprinkle both sides of chops lightly with garlic salt and pepper. Grease bottom of 9 x 13" pan with 2 teaspoons oil and bake pork chops for 30 minutes uncovered at 350 degrees. Turn pork chops over and pour mixture of 1 envelope onion soup, 1½ cups water and mushrooms over chops. Bake uncovered for another 20-30 minutes or until done.

Mother Mable at ninety-one years old. She loved pork chops!

1 cups all purpose flour

½ cup firmly packed light brown sugar

2 teaspoons baking powder

½ teaspoon salt

⅔ cup milk

½ cup lightly salted butter, melted & cooled

2 eggs, lightly beaten

1 teaspoon vanilla

½ cup of each: semisweet chocolate chips, milk chocolate chips, butterscotch chips, peanut butter chips (I sometimes use just 2 kinds of chips, semisweet and peanut butter is really yummy)

⅓ cup chopped walnuts

⅓ chopped pecans

Preheat oven to 400 degrees. Grease twelve muffin cups.

In large bowl, stir together flour, brown sugar, baking powder and salt. In separate bowl stir together milk, butter, eggs, and vanilla until blended. Make a well in center of dry ingredients; add milk mixture and stir just to combine. Stir in chips and nuts.

Spoon batter into prepared muffin cups; bake 15 to 20 minutes or until a toothpick is inserted in center of one muffin comes out clean.

Remove muffin tin to wire rack. Cool 5 minutes before removing muffins from cups then finish cooling on rack. Serve warm or cool completely and store in airtight container at room temperature.

These muffins freeze well. Makes 12 large muffins.

My friend, Karen, who lives in Philadelphia, shared this recipe with me many years ago. Karen has lived in many states and owned and operated catering services. These muffins were one of the best sellers.

I also have served this treat with many variations of the chips, one of my Martha's Tea House favorites.

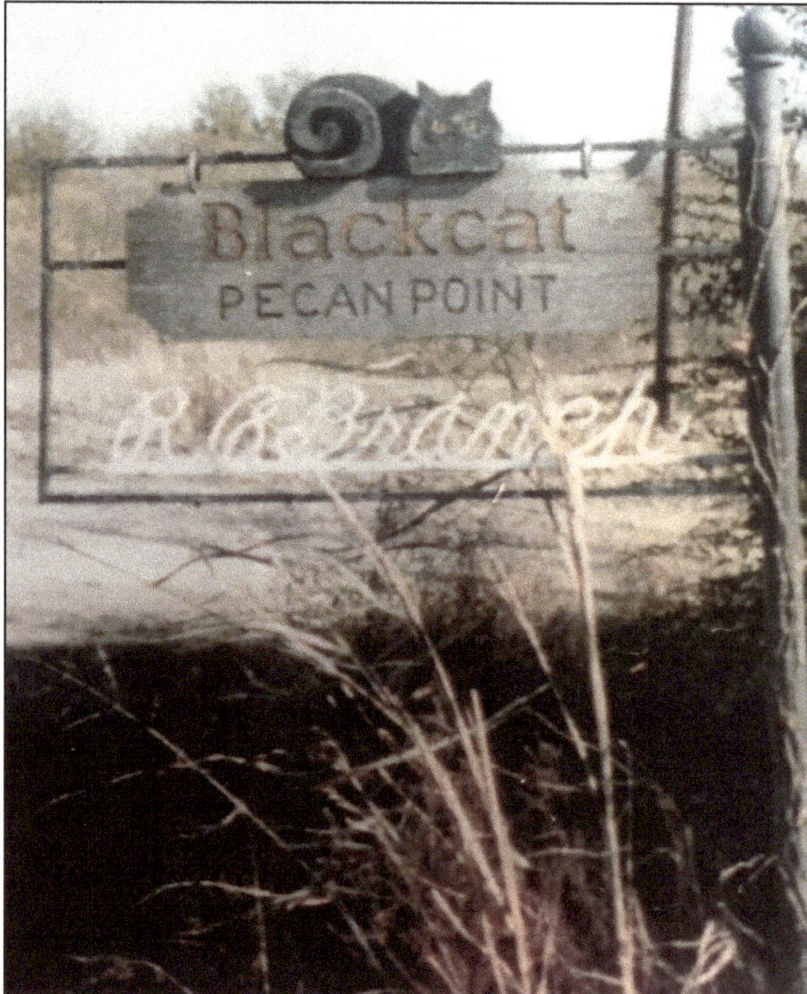

I can see the old two-story house down by the levee, Black Cat, a community located a few miles from Joiner, Arkansas. Mom and Dad lived here when they came from Moulton, Alabama in 1941 to share crop. I was born in this old house on March 31, 1943. We lived downstairs and mother's cousins, Sampson and Lorene Day, lived upstairs. The furnishings weren't much but daddy and mother made the best of it.

They share cropped for several years before moving into Joiner, Arkansas. When I was three years old and Carolyn was about eighteen months old Mother decided our sharecropping days were over. She walked to Joiner, barefoot, with me at her side and Carolyn on her hip. She made a deal with Frank and Anna Mae Felts to buy a lot next to them in Joiner. Daddy was reluctant at first but finally agreed to make the move.

The lot was vacant and bare, no water, no house, no outhouse, no anything! Most of the sharecropping money was spent on the lot which left very few options for housing. Daddy bought a tent and we lived in it for about a year. I remember a few things about the tent. Our beds were on the floor, a big wood burning stove was in the middle of the tent, and we carried water from Roy and Hazel Elrod's house just up the street.

Daddy always liked to work on cars and trucks so he took a job in "Hardhead" Eding's garage, just a few steps from our tent house. Daddy also found a second job working at an oil mill located about five miles away in Wilson, Arkansas. He worked many long hours but never seemed to complain. He would do anything to take care of his family.

A year in the tent was enough! There was finally enough money to buy a house! The house was located in Barge Town, three miles away, and had to be moved to our "tent" lot in Joiner. It consisted of three rooms, shotgun style. We made a living room which doubled as a second bedroom on the front, the middle room had two double beds with a big wood burning stove, and the third room was the kitchen. Daddy added a small room on the back in later years. The ceilings were twelve feet tall and there were two very large bay windows on the front. If Carolyn and I were not playing in those windows we were playing under the house with our friends, Bonnie and Michael Felts. This was fun because the house sat four feet off the ground. We built dirt roads and used our toy trucks and cars to travel to Memphis and Mississippi. Those were the two places we mostly heard about. There was no indoor plumbing so the outhouse remained. Mother washed our clothes in a big black pot in the backyard. I remember her scrubbing our clothes clean on a metal rub board. We took baths in a #2 wash tub. While living here our brother, Wayne, was born.

We had lots of friends in the neighborhood. We played with Susan, Butch, Junior, Johnnie, Connie, and Jerry to name a few. We would stir up some green Kool Aid and play cards on the front porch for hours. We liked to play football and I always wanted to be the quarterback. I usually got my way since I was the only girl the boys would let play. We had talent shows all the time. Some would dance, some would do acrobatics, and some would sing. I was serious about singing. I had lots of practice because I was always performing for my Daddy. If we had company Daddy would pay me a nickel to sing a song for everyone. By the time I finished I had as much as twenty-five cents from my uncles, Percy and Hubert!

When I was twelve years old we moved just up the street to a three-bedroom, one-bath house located next to Daddy's garage. We thought it was a mansion! We had a big front porch and a big back porch. Carolyn, Wayne, and I fought over the bathtub for months before the new wore off and we found so many other adventures we could have in the neighborhood. This is where I lived until age sixteen when I married Alvin Ralph Lloyd. We moved to Kansas City, Missouri, when I was eighteen. I was heartbroken to leave my Mother and Daddy.

I could go on and on but no need for that. I just hope that someday someone can read this and my other stories and have a loving appreciation and understanding of how special your childhood should be.

Share and love your family while you have time.

My Sister Carolyn's Homemade Ice Cream

2 cartons whipping cream

1 can Eagle Brand Milk

1 large can Carnation Milk

1 teaspoon Vanilla

1½ to 2 cups sugar

16 ounces frozen strawberries

2 bananas, chopped

Mix all ingredients together in ice cream freezer, finish filling freezer with milk to the fill line. Use the old fashioned hand freezer or electric freezer to finish the ice cream process. Many fruits can be used. Peaches are a favorite too!

Homemade ice cream out by the pool at Carolyn's house on Sunday with all the family present was the best fun. There was nothing better.

Did you know Thomas Jefferson, Third President of the United States, introduced America to Ice Cream after one of his European excursions.

Busy, busy, busy making all those memories as a child! We never stop to think how many times we will reminisce about those joyful days. Life was really simple and fun.

My Dad was a self-employed mechanic and his garage was located next to our home. You never knew who or when someone would drive in for repair work. It could be a farmer with farm equipment, a black man whose car is broken down on the side of the road, a Mexican who could not speak English but needed his car started, or a driver of a broken down converted school bus that was full of black people from Memphis who had chopped cotton all day and were trying to get home. Daddy was always willing to help anyone, no matter about time of day or which day, he was available.

I loved our little town, located about twenty-five miles from West Memphis, Arkansas on Highway 61. The railroad ran through the middle of town. Joiner consisted of a bus station, two gasoline stations, four grocery stores, movie theater, drug store, a bank, an infamous dairy bar, four dry good stores, a cotton gin, an ice house, furniture store, a first-through-twelfth-grades school, a Baptist Church and a Methodist Church. We had so much to be such a small town! The population was approximately 850 people and everybody knew everybody!

The "infamous dairy bar" arrived! "Hardhead" and Bea Edings introduced the town to the most delicious soft serve ice cream I have ever eaten. I was lucky enough to work there for about a year. I ate so much ice cream! We had a "purple cow" made with NuGrape soda and a "red calf" made with strawberry soda. We also had milkshakes, sundaes, and banana splits. I made them all and I ate them all!

The two gasoline stations were owned by "Hardhead" (W. E.) Edings and Tommy Mooring. "Hardhead" was Daddy's best friend and we actually lived next to their family for several years. "Hardhead" and Bea invited Mother and Daddy to take a trip to Florida with them one year. How exciting was that! Mother and Daddy talked forever about that fun trip! Donald Perry, Wallace Miller, and 2 Chinese families owned the four grocery stores. The Chinese spoke very little English but always had a thriving business. We actually did our grocery shopping at one of the Chinese stores. Shopping was done on Saturday night. Daddy would sit Carolyn, Wayne, and me upon the back of the counter while he and Mother did the shopping. Once we were home we had a party! That one night we were allowed to eat cookies, cakes, lots of sandwiches, and soda pop.

By 9 o'clock everyone was in bed except for Daddy and me. He loved to watch the wrestling on our new television. He would take a little nap then at 10 o'clock I woke him up and we watched the wrestling together. He was hilarious with all his fighting motions!

The dry good stores were owned and operated by Mrs. Faulk, Evenskys, Silversteins, and Baddours. You could buy most any type of clothing, shoes or fabric in any of these stores.

The school was located about one mile from Joiner with twelve grades. There was no kindergarten. The black children had their own school. We never rode the bus. Mother drove us but sometimes we walked home in the afternoon with all the other children.

The Baptist Church was located at one end of the town and the Methodist Church at the other end. We attended the Baptist Church. I always thought it was so big. It is not big but it is a beautiful little church which still looks the same from the outside, sixty years later. John Dresbach was the pianist and I remember learning and singing the books of the Bible while he played. I loved church and looked forward to going. The preacher was Brother Kaffeka and I sat very still and listened. He was so good. I loved all the old hymns and still do. He had a daughter, Sharon Lynn, that was so beautiful and I just idolized her. When my little sister was born in 1959, Mother and Daddy gave me the privilege of naming her Sharon Lynn. I think Sharon Lynn Kaffeka became a writer of children's books.

All of this seems so long ago at times but sometimes I can see all of us playing "kick the can," hide-and-go-seek, football, or rolling tires down the street while being curled up in the center of the tire and another child doing the rolling. We loved to turn fifty-five-gallon drums on the side and walk on them down the street to see who could stay on the longest. We played a lot with toys under our house in the dirt because it was about four feet off the ground and we had plenty of room to stand up under there. Our parents and neighbors sat on Granny Kelly's porch and watched us play in the late afternoon. When it began to get dark we all went inside and got ready for bed. We never had to lock a door when we went to bed in those days.

We go back occasionally to see the few friends that are left. No matter what happens no one can ever take away our fond memories. Joiner, Arkansas will always be a part of my foundation built on Christian principles.

Our little town, Joiner, Arkansas, MY HOME TOWN!

Late August 1949, a day I had dreaded coming for a long time. I was six years old and this was my first day at school! There was no kindergarten, just first through twelfth grades at Shawnee School located in Joiner, Arkansas. The responsibility of "depositing" me to the first grade was assigned to my Aunt Needie, who was a few grades ahead of me. We walked down the LONG hall to the first grade classroom and there stood Mrs. Ray waiting on me. I took one look at this stranger and the huge class room, turned and tightly grabbed my aunt's right leg with my arms and legs and started screaming. I knew they would not make me stay because I was frightened of this "big scary world." I was wrong! I was eventually pried loose from my leg grip and escorted to the classroom. The story doesn't end here. I cried every day for two weeks until Mrs. Ray informed me that I would have to sit in the bathroom all day if the tears did not stop. I was in this "Big Scary World" without my Mother or Daddy but soon realized Mrs. Ray would have her way. I did not want to be locked in the bathroom crying. She won this round, but soon she discovered another dilemma. I was trying to write with my left hand. She tied my left hand in the back of me to try and make me use my right hand. Mrs. Ray lost this battle. I am left handed.

I tell of this first grade experience because this was only the beginning of many "Big Scary Worlds" that I have encountered in my seventy-one years on this beautiful earth. These encounters are out there if you are willing to take the first step and make them happen.

July 11, 1959, sixteen years old and married! I had just finished the tenth grade and now could not go to school married. I cried and cried but finally had to accept it. I obtained employment in a men's shoe factory working on a production line. I worked for Osceola, Arkansas, Shoe Factory for seventeen months.

October 1961 my husband, Alvin Lloyd, secured a job in Kansas City, Missouri. He would be building the tall, blue, A. O. Smith metal silos for farmers in four states: Missouri, Kansas, Nebraska, and Indiana. Yes, traveling all week and gone most weekends. Another day in the "Big Scary World" was moving day to Kansas City and really leaving my Mother, Daddy, and family for the first time. What a heart-breaking scene it was! Standing in our front yard with everyone crying and Alvin tugging at my arm so we could be on our way to a bigger and better world. This was the scene every time we came home for a visit. I love my family so much.

We rented a furnished apartment which was the whole upstairs in a house in Richmond, Missouri, from Beulah McFarland, a widow, whose husband had died in an auto accident. Alvin traveled all the time so "Nanny" and I spent a lot of time together, good times. Summer of 1962, she discovered that I could go to public school married! Nineteen years old and I started back to school in the eleventh grade in Richmond, Missouri! "Big Scary World" was happening to me one more time. I was petrified! My class in Arkansas was only sixteen people, segregated, and here in Richmond the class was one-hundred-fifty-five students, integrated. Nanny and I marched into the school and she made all the arrangements. I was going back to school and I was so happy, but petrified one more time. I had no school clothes or anything else so Nanny bought clothes, shoes, school supplies, and paid for my lunch each week. I rode the school bus because I had just learned to drive and was too scared to venture out of my world. What an experience; I adapted quite well and loved every minute of this new world. I made straight A's!

June 1963, Alvin's job disintegrated and we moved back to Arkansas. He found a job in West Memphis and we were able to buy a little house by using his VA benefits. I enrolled in the twelfth grade in West Memphis and graduated in May 1964. At twenty-one years old I finally had a high school diploma from a public school and had made straight A's! I later attended the University of Memphis, University of Tennessee/ Memphis, and David Lipscomb University in Nashville. In 1979 I became a Real Estate Broker and received many awards for my work with people. After thirty-two years I have retired my real estate license.

I have had some wonderful jobs in my life and, regardless of the type of job, I have always made it a point to do the very best I know how to do by keeping an open mind, helping other people, loving my family and staying positive. I have traveled in thirty-five states and made so many good friends. I am thankful to say that I was able to afford my daughter, Carol, a degree from the University of Memphis. Carol is now forty-three and the Spirit Coordinator, Coach, and Choreographer for the University of Memphis.

I tell all of these things to maybe help someone make difficult decisions in their life, big scary decisions. If I had not gone out into that "Big Scary World" in 1961, I could have been that little Arkansas girl with no education and wasted years. With God's leadership and grace I was saved and enabled to experience so many lovely wonders of this "BIG BEAUTIFUL WORLD."

Step out there, you may stumble a few times but God is always there to pick you up to start over again. Ask for his help. Cream always rises to the top!

Everything you do is based on the choices you make. You and only you are responsible for every decision and choice you make.

"Do not be afraid or discouraged for the Lord your God is with you WHEREVER YOU GO."

Joshua 1:9

Caramel Apple Cider

1 gallon apple cider
1 pound of dark brown sugar
1 pint heavy whipping cream

Heat cider, then add brown sugar. When sugar is melted add whipping cream. Top each serving with additional whipping cream if you like.

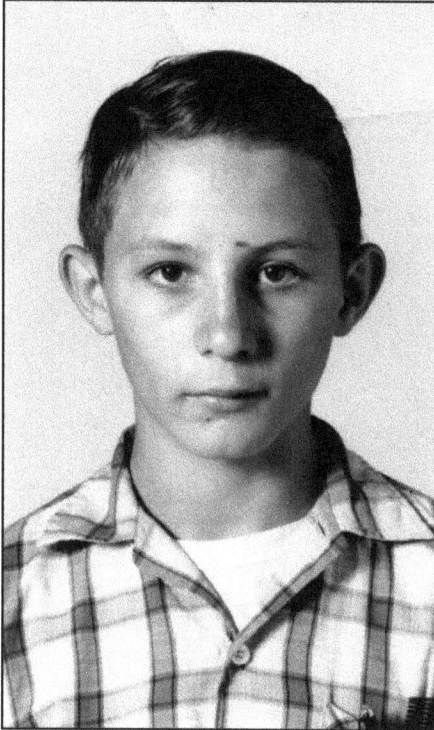

This moment in time was frightful and unforgettable. In 1953, my only brother, Wayne, was five years old. "Prankster Wayne" is a better name. He could create more havoc in one day than all the other children in our neighborhood. Most of the time Wayne played outside in our yard, the neighbor's yard, or sometimes he would wander off for hours trying to find water/mud holes for wading in his bare feet. We would look for him to no avail but he would eventually come home with dirt or mud from head to toe. It didn't bother him to get a spanking because the next day he would set out on a new adventure. My sister Carolyn and I loved to make playhouses and play with our baby dolls. With Wayne around playhouses didn't last long. He could be sweet when he wanted to be but that was 9:00 at night when he was asleep. ☺ Yes, he was filled with mischief and made our lives miserable sometimes but we loved him then and we love him now.

Grandpa and Grandma South lived several miles out in the country on a farm. Their only mode of travel was by horses and wagon. They didn't visit much but we were always excited to see them pulling up in front of our house. We would climb all over the wagon and pet the horses and want to go home with them. When we had family or any visitors we always gathered the wooden straight back chairs for seating and sat around in the front yard underneath a big cottonwood tree.

The Fourth of July was a very hot sunny day so lots of people, including Grandpa and Grandma South came to our house. Mother had made lots of food and everyone was visiting and just enjoying the holiday. Just like today with the Fourth of July we had a few fireworks which consisted of lots of sparklers and a few firecrackers. Daddy was always in charge of the firecrackers and we had great fun with the sparklers. Wayne decided sparklers were not enough for him! He confiscated a few firecrackers. By the time Daddy discovered they were gone and worse yet that Wayne had them, too late!

POW!! Grandma's wooden chair had collapsed and Grandma was on the ground! She was shaken up and couldn't figure out what had just happened. She was a fairly large lovable Grandma so it took several people to rescue her from the ground to a more comfortable chair. It was chaos! But it did not take Daddy very long to figure out what happened. Wayne had lit a firecracker and put it under Grandma's chair! No one saw him do it and he thought it was funny. Fortunately the firecrackers we had at that time were much smaller than today so Grandma did not have any serious injuries. Daddy disappeared a few minutes then emerged from the house with the old trusty razor strap. We knew this was really bad news for Wayne because we had been on the receiving end of this razor strap before and it really hurt! Yes, Wayne got a terrible whipping and had to hug Grandma's neck and tell her he was so sorry. He was confined to the house for the rest of the day's activities.

Late afternoon and our Grandparents had to be home before dark. We always hated to see them leave because we loved them so much and their visits were special.

Do you have a Grandpa and Grandma? Spend time with them, tell them you love them, and hug, hug, hug them all you can. They are wise people, listen to them and encourage them to share their life stories with you. You will be sharing their stories — and yours — with your children someday.

Mid 1950's, hot summer days in the neighborhood and lots of time for playing. Playing, what's that? Playing is about the most fun you can have on a summer day. Out of school, barefoot, popsicles, Kool Aid, ice cream, and all your neighborhood friends gathering round to decide what game everyone wants to play. We had so many choices of games and so many yards in which to have fun. One day it might be Granny Kelly's front yard, next day a front porch, the big vacant lot behind Daddy's garage, or maybe in the middle of the street! Yes, we were all creative and the games could last for hours.

We played many of the usual games like Hide-and-Go-Seek and Kick-the-Can. Granny Kelly's front yard was the location of the can to be kicked. One playmate was in charge of protecting the can and everyone else found a hiding place. The purpose was for a player to try and kick the can while the person in charge was looking for all the other players. Once the can was kicked all the players grouped, repositioned the can and the game started again. We usually had an audience sitting on Granny Kelly's porch who enjoyed our games, especially when we were playing Hide-and-Go-Seek. We liked to play this game in the late afternoon so we could extend it past dark (easier to hide— harder to find). By this time the Moms, Dads, and babies were sitting on Granny Kelly's porch, laughing, talking, and watching us hide. Once all the players were found, the game started over with a different person being the seeker. Can't children play these games today, priceless and lots of fun.

Summers were long and there was plenty of time for baseball, football, track, basketball, and bicycles. My favorite activity was always the talent show. A grassy area blocked off in the corner of the vacant lot was the stage. Everyone gathered around the stage to watch the performers. Acrobats, dancers, whistlers, and singers did their best and had fun. I always sang a song like "Cross over the Bridge," "I Have a Boyfriend," or "Secret Love," because I sang for my Dad all the time. If someone had a birthday we all sang "Happy Birthday."

Our paved street was one lane and had very little traffic. Daddy had several fifty-five-gallon empty drums at his garage so we moved the barrels to the center of the street, turned them to the side, climbed upon the barrels and proceeded to walk them down the street, turned around and walked them back up the street where someone else would have a turn. Some of the best times I ever had! The second game we played in the street was rolling and racing old worn out tires up and down the street to see who could roll the fastest. Didn't cost a penny, nobody was hurt, and a hot soapy bath took care of the dirt and grime.

So many games I could talk about, "Annie Over," "Red Rover," "Ring Around the Roses," to name just a few. But by this time you probably think I'm nuts.

What about putting away the electronics and giving the children's fingers a rest? Explore, discover, and enjoy our big beautiful world. It is waiting for you OUTSIDE.

Hot Chocolate

3 cups milk
3 cups half-and-half
2 cups milk chocolate chips

Heat the milks, add chocolate chips, stir until melted. Serve with whipping cream if you like.

Oh, the pleasant safe feeling one can feel walking into your home after being away for one day, one month, or one year. I experienced these feelings at an early age. I identified with coming home and knowing I was safe and happy. Let me tell you this story.

Daddy and Mother worked hard to support our family. In the summer time, work was slow for Daddy in the garage. We had cousins who had been traveling to Michigan for several years to pick fruit and vegetables during the summer. Daddy thought this was a great idea for us. I don't think Mother liked it but she didn't say much. She would do whatever it took to make a living for a family of six.

The first of June, Daddy closed his garage and we prepared the home to be vacant for six to eight weeks. We loaded clothes, dishes, linens, anything we thought we would need to survive for the next two months and I do mean survive! We traveled to Keeler, Michigan, 700 miles. We stayed in a one-room cabin, approximately 10' x 12' and worked from 5 AM until dark, six and seven days a week. I remember sitting on the end of the strawberry rows waiting for daylight so we could see to pick the berries and place in the eight-quart carriers. We were paid eight cents a quart for picking and ten cents a quart for taking off the green stems.

After four weeks, the strawberry picking was over but Mother would can quarts and quarts for us to haul back to Arkansas for strawberry pies in the winter time.. Next were the raspberries, stickers everywhere! We hated it but this was over in about two weeks. We tried to pick gooseberries but only a half day. The thorns were treacherous and Mother decided we were not going through that torture. Was it time to go home? No! We had to pick cherries. The trees were tall which called for long ladders for clearing the top limbs. The tree had to be completely cleared of any fruit before you could go to the next tree. I was always scared Daddy would fall. We could usually make it through the cherry picking pretty good because we could see the light at the end of the tunnel. We were going home! The finality of two long months of hard work, we could hardly wait to get home! Hurry up Daddy, we want to play before school starts!

The most amazing person on this excursion was my Mother. She cooked two, sometimes three meals a day, on a two-burner oil stove and portable oven, plus worked all day with us in the fields. We had homemade biscuits, eggs, oatmeal, corn beef hash or bacon every day for breakfast. For supper, we always had a balanced meal complete with homemade biscuits or cornbread.

We usually had store-bought cookies or cakes for dessert. She cooked the meals and washed the dishes. We simply "washed up" and got ready for bed. 4 AM came early. We only took a bath on Saturday afternoons because there was no indoor plumbing.

We loved it when Daddy said "It's time to go home."

We really had a home to go to. So many of the people we worked with were full-time migratory workers and did not have a home. Fourteen hours travel time, but we were ready to sleep in our own beds. Upon arrival we could hardly wait for Daddy to unlock the front door! We would all crowd in and wander through each room like we had never seen it before. The rooms always seemed larger, the furniture was beautiful and we fought over who would get the bathtub first. We bathed three times a day for a long time! Baths were such a luxury we had taken for granted. Nothing compares to sleeping in your own bed. Oh yes! The television, we couldn't watch it enough. Lord, it was good to be home! We had two weeks before school started to rest, relax, and contact all of our friends in the neighborhood. We could go barefoot, ride our bicycles, play hide-and-go-seek, and just be a kid! I loved our little town. It was a safe place to be happy and loved.

Can you identify with this story? Home is so special, don't take it for granted. Listen to me. Make everything special, your home, your life, your children, your friends, and loved ones. When they are gone they are gone forever. You can't bring them back. Show your love and enjoy your life's excursions.

May 1, 2017

I was only sixteen and she was twenty-six when Alberta came to our home the very first time. She was beautiful, polite and very quiet. Sometimes you just meet that special person that feels like family. This is what happened. Our family embraced her and we knew Alberta would be a welcomed addition to our family.

Alberta met our Uncle Hubert Sparks while working in an orange processing plant in 1958 in Bartow, Florida. They happened to be "clocking in" for work at the same time. She was smitten with him that very moment and they were married Valentine's Day, February 14, 1959.

Aunt Alberta was born September 27, 1933. She tells me that she was the shy one of the three siblings. Growing up in Fort Meade were happy days. Her Dad had a workshop in the backyard where he taught welding during war time. The nation was recovering from the Depression and World War II so he also worked with Civil Defense. During this scary time of air raid warnings he was in charge of sounding the siren and making sure all lights were out in the town of Fort Meade, Florida. Stamp and Ration Books were issued. Rations included sugar, coffee, tea, shortening, even gas. Aunt Alberta says they never went hungry. She does remember wearing "handmade bloomers" that her Mom made from rubber inner tubes.

School was always special to Aunt Alberta, especially high school. Once a month, she and the remaining classmates, usually about six, gather in Bartow, a few miles from home, to visit and talk about the good old days.

Historical Fort Meade, Florida, was a busy little town with lots of grocery stores, theater, pharmacy, bank, café with curb service, bakery, Coca Cola plant, and a corner drug store for enjoying double dips of ice cream. The bank was once robbed and the robbers were apprehended on her grandfather's land. He also owned the local blacksmith shop where he ground corn for grits and corn meal. As a little girl, Aunt

Alberta remembers feeding baby calves with baby bottles of milk, but one of her favorite things to do was to play with the baby chickens. Her Grandma Minnie owned a goat and a cow. She would make goat milk ice cream and always had fresh churned butter. After trading in town on Saturday night, Aunt Alberta and her Mama would walk home and always stopped on the same little path to sit and eat cheese puffs. Just another good time she remembers. ☺

After Aunt Alberta and Uncle Hubert were married they spent a little time in Michigan working as migratory workers. They soon moved to Arkansas but Aunt Alberta missed her family and wanted to move back to Florida. Uncle Hubert gathered and sold pecans for enough money to return to Florida to live and raise their family.

Landscaping and gardening were Uncle Hubert's passion. He worked for the "Great Masterpiece" in Lake Wales, Florida. A large mosaic picture of the Last Supper was the main attraction. There was a large movie screen, restaurant, ski lift tours, and zoo animals. Uncle Hubert would travel to Busch Gardens to transport bears to the resort for vacationers viewing.

So many sweet stories, I wish I could tell them all! Aunt Alberta Maye and Uncle Hubert Sanders Sparks shared an undying and enduring love for each other during their marriage. They were a beautiful couple who always "stuck together." Uncle Hubert was a tall, thin handsome guy who sang and played the guitar his whole life. Aunt Alberta plays the piano and is loved by all. She has always been the special aunt in our family. She told me about the warm welcome and love she felt the first time she came to our home, the Johnnie and Mable South family home in Joiner, Arkansas.

Uncle Hubert and Aunt Alberta have four children: Judy, Bobby (who has gone on to be with the Lord), Angela, and Andy. This sweet man, father, husband, and fabulous uncle was born on January 9, 1928, and passed on January 15, 2004. He is buried in the Evergreen Cemetery in Fort Meade, Florida, just down the street from their family home.

Aunt Alberta is eighty-three years old and lives with her daughter, Judy in Fort Meade. She is truly the "Queen Bee" of this family. She is surrounded with grandchildren and great grandchildren galore who come by every day to visit with her. What a treat that must be! ☺

Everybody in the South Family loves and misses you — Beautiful Lady, Aunt Alberta Maye Bobbett Sparks. You have always been and always will be my favorite Aunt. You have helped to create some beautiful memories for all of us. Your trip to Tennessee and my home are forever etched into my memory. We had such a good time, so many fun things with the family!

My Uncle Hubert was always full of surprises for me. He traveled from Florida to Arkansas then to Michigan three or four times a year. Our home in Joiner, Arkansas, was the only place he called home. We never knew when he would make an appearance but he was always welcome as long as he wanted to stay. I loved my Uncle Hubert and I always liked to see him show up because he never failed to bring a surprise gift for me. Uncle Hubert was my Mother's brother and he loved playing the guitar. Sometimes he, my Mother, and I would sing while he played. It was obvious that I was his favorite of four children because no one else received a special treat. I especially liked for him to return after his trips to Florida because the gifts from the sunshine state were always a magical delight for me.

In the summer of 1953, when I was nine years old, Uncle Hubert was at our home after a short trip to Florida. You never knew how long he would stay. Sometimes his visit would be a week and other times one or two months. I had no idea what my surprise was going to be but I saw the wrapped box with a bow and I just knew it was really going to be grand. I tried to guess but it was impossible and I knew he wouldn't tell me. He wanted for me to open the box when all the family was present. This part was a challenge because my Daddy worked all the time on one or two jobs. I can see the family gathered on a Sunday morning in the living room anxiously awaiting the reveal. I looked at the box one more time and began to tear, rip, and pull the bow and wrapping paper from the box revealing a beauteous eye-catching cedar treasure chest! The lid and front were adorned with carvings of flowers and a beautiful serene picture of a church surrounded by mountains decorated the center of the chest. Inside the chest was a picture of movie actress, Gale Storm. She was my favorite actress who starred in a popular television sitcom called "My Little Margie." I loved the picture and was so excited about the treasure chest! I could think of a million things to store in this keepsake for use in my playhouse. The smile on Uncle Hubert's face was one of the biggest I had ever seen from him. He knew he had made me happy.

Today is December 4, 2019, and guess what? The Treasure Chest is sitting on the desk in my sun room. This little treasure chest, 14 x 8 x 6 inches, is even more beautiful today. Through the years the chest has survived the playhouses, marbles, jacks, baby doll clothes, popsicle sticks, and nickels and dimes I collected from singing for my Daddy and Uncle Hubert.

Why am I so excited about this Treasure Chest? It's the little things that count in life. We all have a treasure chest, spelled "HEART." Fill it full with happy thoughts and memories of our loved ones. More time is not promised in our big beautiful world. Take the one chance you are given and live for the Lord.

"God will work for you; you need only to be still."

Exodus 14:14

5 o'clock on a Sunday morning and mother is yelling at Daddy. There is no flour in the house for Mother to make her scratch biscuits and chocolate gravy for our Sunday morning special breakfast, our favorite of the week. Traditional food shopping was always completed on Saturday night at the Chinaman's grocery store in Joiner after Daddy closed the garage for the weekend. Somehow flour never made it to the list or the counter where all supplies were piled for checkout. The dilemma meant no bread of any kind in the house for our Sunday breakfast. We ate our scrambled eggs, bacon, and jelly in silence. Why not go to the grocery store on Sunday morning to purchase the flour or a loaf of bread? For many years there was no establishment open on Sunday to buy anything. That was the law. Sunday was a day of total rest. If you had worked in the cotton fields, driven farm equipment all week, daily traipsed on a factory floor, or worked in a garage for six straight days, then you were glad to have this welcome break.

The most favorite thing to do on Sunday as a family was attend, watch, and participate in stock car races in Blytheville, Arkansas, about forty miles from home in Joiner. I say participate in the car races because our Daddy owned a race car, Good Old Number 7! We chose seven to represent the number of people who lived in our home. (Most of the time only six but Uncle Hubert would show up and stay two or three months at a time so we included him). Daddy always had two drivers at the races in case one was a "no show" but both would be there fussing over who was to be the driver that Sunday. Uncle Hubert Sparks was one driver and Pete Canady, a friend of the family, was the second. They were not just drivers of this special machine, the winner's circle came often for this Number 7 car! Daddy would get so excited and always insisted on his family being part of the fun and excitement.

We also attended the rodeo in Osceola, about eighteen miles from home when the car racing season had ended. There were the usual bull riding and bucking horse events but they had pony rides for the children before the rodeo started. Ice cream and soda pop just completed these Sunday outings.

Sunday was always like a weekly holiday. If there was no car race or rodeo, then after breakfast and church we were off to our aunts and uncles who lived in the country. The many cousins were always glad to see us. We would have lunch but we were always anxious to get the playing started. The women and men gathered under a big shade tree in the front yard to talk and watch their children having fun. In the winter we assembled in the kitchen to play cards, jacks, or any game we could play without getting into mischief. Televisions were very scarce so we entertained ourselves. By 5:00 in the afternoon Daddy wanted to go home, take a short nap, and prepare for the Monday workday. Sunday was coming to a close once again.

"Closed on Sunday" was known as the "Blue Law," which was practiced until the early 1970s. Everyone adapted to this rule of conduct which quite often required a bit more discipline than one liked. This law was enforced by a governing authority and respected by all. These weekly holidays hold so many special memories, especially since our Mother and Daddy are gone. Sometimes I feel so very alone but all I have to do is conjure up some of these beautiful childhood moments and I realize how much I love my family and know that I am not alone.

"I am a child of God."

Deuteronomy 23:5

"Sugar and spice and everything nice, that's what little girls are made of." Nothing goes better with sugar and spice than baby dolls, tea parties, and playhouses. Where can this baby doll, tea party, and playhouse event take place? It could be in the corner of a bedroom, in the yard, on the playground, or anywhere the imagination can take you. Often times, there is a real playhouse that someone has constructed which includes windows, doors, and even a front porch. Some playhouses even have furniture which includes a bed for the special guest, the baby dolls. Hours of fond memories await that special little girl. Sometimes while driving I see a backyard playhouse and I am always tempted to stop and look for baby dolls and little girls enjoying a tea party in their special house.

I think about the many playhouses I have enjoyed through the years. One of the best was with my sister, Carolyn. We had a chicken house at the back of our property that Carolyn and I played in and around. Boards, barrels, bricks, cans, and sticks were some of the things we stored for our imaginary play sessions. One particular day we really used our imagination. The rain came one night but the sun showed up in the morning and it was playhouse time for us! Our playhouse came to life when we set up the boards on the bricks to make the imaginary walls and the barrels became our table with cans turned upside down for stools to set on. We had been saving our popsicle sticks for a special occasion and this was it! The dirt we always played in had become mud from the rain, the thick black kind, perfect for fudge-sicles and mud pies. We formed the "chocolate" mud pies and stuck the sticks in the fudge-sicles then let them dry. Needless to say we couldn't find anyone to try them, not even the baby dolls. Carolyn and I decided to taste, it was awful! They looked pretty but looks were deceiving that day.

Our family traveled to Michigan in the summer time for many years to pick fruit. We lived in small cabins, usually located in an apple or cherry orchard. I always looked for a place to play when we were not working in the strawberry fields or cherry orchards. I discovered an abandoned milk truck close to our cabin that had a missing door and broken windows. I swept it clean and I knew I had found the perfect playhouse. I gathered any and everything I could find including my mother's skillet to do my pretend cooking and make my baby doll comfortable. I used a towel for a bed for the baby doll's naps and a strawberry crate to sit on and play with her. I had some happy hours. This playhouse moment happened over fifty years ago but I can still perfectly imagine it.

As the years have passed many changes have come about in my life but my love for playhouses has never diminished. My husband, Eddie Cooke, and I live on the family farm. On this farm, close to our home, is a very old "little house" that his Aunt Sarah Belle lived in for many years. The house is approximately 700 square feet with a big living room-bed room combination, and a kitchen, breakfast area, and bathroom in the back. When we moved here the little house was full of furniture, clothes, shoes, and junk. My husband gave me this little house to create whatever I wanted to. It was Playhouse time again! I started by filling up a 32' dumpster to get rid of the junk. I sifted through and salvaged some of the remaining items to use in my playhouse. Once the cleaning was finished I then completed the painting. You should see it! The ceiling is constructed of 4'x8' sheets of plywood and I have painted each section with a different color of paint. The walls have been sectioned and painted red, green, yellow, blue, and one section with hot air balloon wallpaper. The bathroom and kitchen were refurbished with new flooring and new equipment. I am constantly changing the décor but I have a few antiques and of course Baby Dolls that will always be a part of my life.

I share my playhouse with many people. It is actually used for a guest house, Bible study meetings, luncheons, or just any kind of fun get together. September 1, 2012, we had a wedding for a young couple from our church. The bride and her five bridesmaids were guests in my playhouse for the night before the wedding. The wedding was performed at 5:00 in the afternoon under a big oak tree in the middle of the pasture with two hundred guests sitting on hay bales. Such a sweet ceremony and blessing for everyone. The happy couple and all their out-of-town guests danced the night away on the large backyard patio while the DJ spun the favorite songs. Everyone had fun and the wedding was perfect. I have so much fun myself with decorating, reading, or just sitting and thinking how blessed I really am. From a dilapidated old milk truck playhouse as a little girl to a Real Honest-to-Goodness Playhouse at seventy years old and sharing my life with my husband on the family farm. Dreams do come true.

Thank you Lord.

"God hears your prayers." Call upon me and pray to me and I will hear you."

Jeremiah 29:12

Greek Soup

      1 pound lean ground beef, browned and drained
      1 can Rotel, original
      1 can diced tomatoes (14.5 oz)
      1 can Spanish rice (approx. 15 oz.)
      1 can Veg All (approx. 15 oz.)
      2 teaspoons Greek seasoning
      $1^3/_4$ cups water

Mix all ingredients in crockpot and cook on high 30 minutes then reduce to low for 2 hours. Serves 6 – 8 people. I always double this recipe for tea parties.

My sister, Carolyn, worked for General Motors for thirty years. She shared this easy soup recipe many years ago. They made Greek soup at work. Each of the employees brought 1 ingredient for the soup. Upon arrival to work the crockpot was filled with all the tasty flavors. Lunch was ready in 2 - 3 hours and served with crackers.

Today we hear about so many children that are being mistreated, abandoned or stolen. Have you ever really wondered what it would be like for your child to be stolen? Gone and possibly never returning or not knowing whether they are dead or alive? Can you imagine the panic, desperation and heartache a parent must feel?

I had an incident that happened with my little girl, Carol Ann, and me. I could never forget this agonizing experience. I still sometimes cry.

My husband and I had built our dream home in the Arkansas countryside in 1970, just north of West Memphis. Our home was located on four acres in the middle of a bean field and fronting on a gravel road. Our neighbor, Mrs. Chappell, lived about three-hundred yards away across an overgrown acre of land with a tall hedgerow. She was a lonely little lady who visited Carol Ann and me quite often.

On a hot July day, Mrs. Chappell was chatting with me in my kitchen while I was canning green beans. Carol was just outside the kitchen window playing with her toys. I would look out the window every few minutes and she seemed to be having a good time. Then, on my next glance, there was no Carol Ann!

I ran outside calling for her but there was no response. I looked all around the house and still couldn't find my baby! My heart was racing and a sick feeling was swelling up in the pit of my stomach but my mind was saying don't panic. I ran as many of the bean field rows as I could, thinking I would find her, but there was no Carol. I ran to the gravel road in front of the house, looking, screaming, and running both directions but still no Carol. All I could think was someone had come along and taken my three-year-old baby!

As a last resort I raced through the tall weeds, bean field, and hedge row to Mrs. Chappell's house. I burst through the back door running and yelling and there in Mrs. Chappell's living room, sitting on the sofa was My Carol! What a welcome sight! Carol started laughing and I started crying. She was playing hide and seek and didn't even know it. The moment I saw her I felt relief, joy, peace, and even a little bit of anger. I hugged and kissed and hugged and kissed my baby girl and so did Mrs. Chappell. We were so glad to see her and know she was safe.

I could not imagine being without my baby Carol. I shared the experience with my husband that night and cried even more. He put his arms around me to let me know everything was all right.

This day was an unforgettable learning and agonizing experience. Hold onto your children and appreciate them whether big or small. They can be gone in a heartbeat!

"He fills my life with good things."

Psalm 103:5

Often times we are looking for the big happenings in our lives while very special every day events go unnoticed. Years later we say "Do you remember" or "That was really special when," constantly wishing we had the opportunity to bring back those special moments. One such time I remember well.

My husband and I had talked about going somewhere to have a picnic. Not just any picnic, a special event. We lived in the Arkansas country, about twenty-five miles north of West Memphis in 1974. Carol was about three years old and loved her Daddy's horses. We had a buggy and a horse named King that loved to pull the buggy. Our picnic was to be at a small lake located eight miles from our home and we were traveling by horse and buggy.

My husband was always excited about anything we did which included horses. He was awake bright and early that Sunday morning preparing the horse and buggy for our family outing. I prepared the picnic lunch with many tasty treats, including pork & beans, which my husband always liked. Carol took her favorite baby doll, Beanie. We were all set for a day of fun and relaxation.

The summer day was beautiful, lots of sunshine, birds singing, rabbits in the fields, and lots of squirrels. We were having fun! We traveled all the back roads to avoid the interstate but even on this road were spectators. Some of them just curious, some were excited to see the horse and buggy and a lot of them wanted a short ride. We just responded with a friendly hello and a moment for them to pet King and look at the buggy. We were in no big hurry and seeing a horse and buggy was unusual in that part of Arkansas. Time was not important on this day, we were not on a schedule and it was our family day.

I don't remember how long we traveled but we arrived at the lake. A few people were fishing but no one else had a picnic. Carol Ann and I played and walked and Alvin took a short nap.

When we left we returned by a different route. We traveled a few back roads then took the service road next to Interstate 55. This route created a traffic jam several times. The interstate traffic slowed and people stared and honked their horns. They wanted to be a part of our special day. We just waved, smiled, and continued our homeward journey. Carol was so excited when we did get home and her Dad sat her upon King and walked around the bean field for a long time next to our home. King was a gentle horse and a member of our family for many years.

A special day that seemed to come and go in a moment. We take too many things for granted. This beautiful day is stored in my memory bank and I continue to recall it quite often. If only I could re-live it with my baby and husband. We had so much in life and so much fun that day. I am thankful for the pleasant memories. Thank you, Lord.

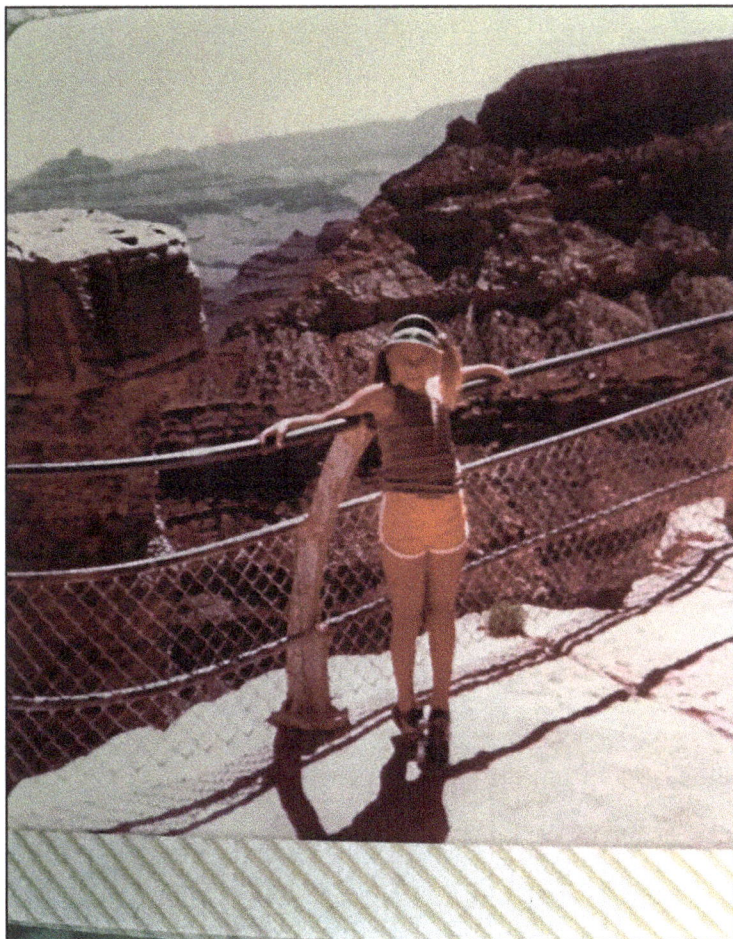

Carol at the Grand Canyon

Have you ever allowed yourself to dream? How big are your dreams? Do you settle for small, vague imaginativeness or do you stretch beyond your fears and explore the windmills of your creativeness? Believe in yourself, conjure up a vision and make it a real life occurrence. For dreams to come true you have to set fear aside. Press forward with positive thoughts, beliefs and a realization that you can make it happen.

This one time I would hate to know that I had not been fearless and determined enough to press forward and experience an unforgettable treasured vacation. In 1978, when Carol was seven years old, my husband and I had many discussions about a special extended family holiday. We finally quit talking about it and on Saturday, June 3, 1978, 7:30 AM, we drove out of the driveway with our loaded pop-up camper attached. We set out for a real adventure, no itinerary or time table. We wanted to see sights we had only heard, dreamed, or read about. As soon as we were on the road I started a "journal" (legal size lined sheets of paper) to chronicle our "Magic Carpet Ride."

We decided to drive west and the first night was spent in Mt. Pleasant, Texas, sleeping in our pop-up camper and enjoying a picnic. We traveled on through Texas to New Mexico. There we experienced the self-guided 1½ mile tour of Carlsbad Caverns and watched the bats fly out at 7:30 PM. The stalactites and stalagmites were a real wonder but they are only for viewing, no touching until the end of the tour in a designated area.

We traveled to Artesia and through a beautiful little community called Cloudcroft, New Mexico. The elevation was 9,000 feet and we were literally in the clouds (close to heaven ☺). My husband finally pulled me away and we were headed toward La Cruces then into Alamogordo. A zoo in the middle of a park in Alamogordo was a welcome sight for another picnic. After shopping and buying pinatas we were on our way to see the White Sands National Monument located about twenty miles from Alamogordo.

Deming, New Mexico, here we come! My husband and I wanted to see this little town, 7000 population. We pondered the thought of buying some land here many years ago. I'm glad we didn't! We kept driving and I know we saw at least 10,000 cacti and yuccas and the mountains were just unbelievable!

Our next stop was Willcox, Arizona, home of Rex Allen. Wilcox is close to Benson which sits in a valley with beautiful mountains all around. We were up and down the mountains, hard on the ears. ☺ We had never seen so many house trailers (mobile homes) as there were in all the small towns.

We stopped in Tucson for food and gas then continued through Gila Bend, Arizona where the temperature was 115 degrees at 3:15 PM! There were beautiful cotton crops, with irrigation, everywhere. When we arrived in Yuma the temperature was still 115 degrees so we stayed in the Holiday Inn. The next day we traveled through Brawley, California, 106 degrees with thousands of bales of hay alongside the highway, with fields of cotton and alfalfa everywhere.

We were at sea level and began to travel through the mountains again. San Diego was one hundred miles away. Cocktail lounges highly advertised on radio and billboards, opening at 8:00 AM. We stopped at Pine Valley in the mountains, fifty miles from San Diego. This small community had all the makings of small town—family living with banks, schools, doctors, shopping, and even pastures with horses. Most of the residents drive to San Diego to work which is ninety percent mountainous driving!

San Diego was next and we decided to stay here for the night. We visited Balboa Park and Zoo. We left the next morning for Los Angeles. We drove the Pacific scenic route 21. See it to believe it! Oil wells in the middle of Huntington Beach and really all along the beach as we traveled.

We drove to Anaheim, California, and decided to stay in a hotel. We visited Disneyland and rode everything! Knotts Berry Farm, Hollywood Wax Museum, and Universal Studios rounded out the two-day exploration.

My husband's company had a branch office in Long Beach so our next stop was to visit with the manager and employees for a few hours. At this point we had driven 2,479 miles and we knew where we were going when we left here, the Grand Canyon!

Williams, Arizona, is located about fifty miles from the Grand Canyon. We stayed here and toured this magnificent wonder the next day. If you visit a hundred times you can never grow tired of experiencing God's wonder here. You can hike to the bottom by yourself or take the mule ride for $75 per person which includes night lodging, food, and the return trip next day. Daytime temperature was in the 80s but at night in the 40s. The Indian jewelry is the most beautiful and reasonably priced. My husband surprised me with a unique and beautiful keepsake turquoise ring. We could have stayed several days but a new adventure was calling.

We were on the road again headed toward Albequerque, New Mexico. We detoured and visited the Petrified Forest and the Painted Desert. These sites were worth the detour.

Seeing is believing! We are in Gallup, New Mexico, and there are Indians everywhere! They all had on either a black or white hat. Bars were all along the street and there were no sober Indians. I wanted to take pictures but I was scared to roll down the window! We were within six feet of all the action. ☺ No, we did not stay, we drove on to Amarillo and slept at the Holiday Inn.

Oklahoma City here we come! We toured the Cowboy Hall of Fame and visited that night a couple of hours with an old friend, Jane Sage. She had not seen us in several years so that made our Oklahoma City tour even more special.

Hopefully you can read between the lines, enjoy the tours and maybe have a little laugh along the way while you read my story. We traveled 3,762 miles and I've wanted to write about this twenty-one-day "Treasured Moments" for several years but could not figure out how to approach it. There is so much more to this story. Many more stops along the way, just the way life is but my prayer is that you glean at least one blessing from my heartfelt story. You see, my husband, Alvin, has since died, and my daughter, Carol Ann, is now forty-six years old. This was truly just a moment in time and moments are all we have.

Johnny Wayne, my brother, wading in the mud puddles.

Daddy aggravating Aunt Needie by pulling on her big toes.

"Hardhead," Daddy's best friend, vigorously rubbing his hands together while laughing.

Having hands small enough for washing fruit jars.

Peeling peaches while sitting underneath the Mimosa tree in Granny and Pa Edings front yard.

All the family being at the kitchen table together for every evening meal.

Mother making homemade biscuits or cornbread every meal.

Waiting until Christmas morning to open all the gifts.

Picking strawberries in Michigan in our special four-quart carriers made by Daddy and having to go to bed at 6:00 PM so we could be up by 4:00 AM to pick more strawberries each day.

The big crepe myrtle in our front yard that Mother loved.

The Sunday dinners Mother prepared. Pork chops, chicken, and spaghetti for one meal and everyone being there to share.

Playing under our old house with Carolyn, Michael, and Bonnie Felts.

Carolyn and I making mud pies and putting popsicle sticks in them to pretend they were fudge treats.

Carolyn stepping in hot ashes in our backyard and big blisters popping up on her feet.

That mischievous little Wayne, our brother, placing a button up his nose and having to rush him to the hospital in Memphis to have it removed.

Carolyn, Wayne, and I having the chicken pox at the same time.

The clock that Daddy gave Mother for Christmas with the "pretend" fireplace that lit up when the clock was plugged in.

Playing "hide-and-go-seek" and "kick-the-can" until dark while Mother, Daddy, Pa and Granny Kelly, Bea and Hardhead and Collis and Gertineal sat on Granny Kelly's porch talking and watching us have fun.

Bea and Hardhead bringing the wonder of the Dairy Bar ice cream to our town, Joiner.

Paying eight cents to attend a Saturday afternoon movie or any other day.

How Carolyn and I hated to pick cotton, made me ill to think about it.

The coat Mother purchased at a rummage sale in Hartford, Michigan for twenty-five cents and I had to wear for three years! Carolyn wore it two years after me!

The day Wayne, as a small child, found Daddy's gun, pointed it at me and said he was going to shoot!

The morning Mother and Daddy told us Grandpa South had died at John Gaston Hospital in Memphis.

The day my little sister Sherry was born. I adored and helped Mother take care of her. I named her Sharon Lynn South.

How Mother and Daddy never spoke a harsh word to each other when we were little children.

The time Sherry had Hepatitis in the third grade, almost lost her!

The feelings of love, happiness, and security that abounded in our family.

Mother making us stay all those nights in a dark, musty storm cellar to escape thunderstorms. Scary!

Hearing Daddy pray.

The night my Daddy died…

The streets are so short and narrow. The houses are worn, torn and tired. Swoosh, a feather has just knocked over another dilapidated building. How did the trees get so big! You can hardly see clearly down the street because tree limbs meet in the middle of the streets and block the beautiful sunrays. Where is the meadow where we loved to play games and make bracelets and necklaces from the clover tops? Four leaf clovers could be plucked by the handful. Where are the mud holes all the children enjoyed after a hot steamy afternoon shower? Where are all the children? Sad.

Why don't we ride our bicycles up the street to the Dairy Bar for an ice cream treat. I'll race you! Oh, but the Dairy Bar has been replaced by grass, dirt, and gravel. Let's cross the street to Hardhead's Texaco station and buy a Coca Cola with our nickel weekly allowance. One look and you see the faded blue Texaco building, barely standing with no windows or doors. What a treat it would be to have a five cent Coca Cola today! Middle of the day and the theatre is not open yet but we could check out which western will be showing this Saturday. We only need eight cents to enjoy the movie with all our friends. The fun and excitement of Saturday afternoon movies are no more. The movie theatre and Banks Drug Store next door have been gone for eons.

Let's go to the empty lot behind Daddy's garage and play some football. I want to be the quarterback! Oh, there is no empty lot. A house trailer now occupies this playground. Where is our basketball goal that reigned over our backyard by Daddy's garage? School is starting soon and I want to be a basketball star this year in 9th grade. I need to practice! No basketball goal, no backyard, and no South Family house, but the crepe myrtle that Mother loved is still out front unattended. I see Granny and Pa Edings sitting underneath their mimosa tree in the front yard shelling purple hull peas, let's go help them. There are no purple hull peas to shell and no peaches to peel and slice. Our Granny and Pa Edings are gone to be with the Lord.

Let's all jump on our bikes and ride down the road past Buck Wilson's house to our school, Shawnee. I'll be the leader so follow me. We could play on the monkey bars for a little while before we have to go home for supper. But, wait a minute, look! No monkey bars, no playground, no school are anywhere to be seen. Shawnee School was torn down several years ago to leave only open spaces.

I tell you all of this because Joiner, Arkansas, is my hometown and most of it has faded into the past. Joiner was such a happy little town, 850 population, and you knew everybody. You never had to lock your doors or hide your vehicles in a garage. It was a safe haven for all the children wherever they wanted to play. The population sign now reads 576.

Joiner First Baptist Church recently celebrated their 75th anniversary. I was so excited to be able to attend. My husband, Eddie, and I spent the night at Marion which is about fifteen minutes from Joiner. We arrived in Marion mid-afternoon on Saturday. We visited the cemetery in Marion where my Mother, Daddy and a few other family members are buried and placed flowers on each grave.

The celebration started at 11:00 AM, so early Sunday morning we traveled to Joiner to tour the little town before going to the church. This "Moment in Time" describes the current scenes in my little hometown. I was sad when I saw it but all the sweet, fun memories came flooding back and washed all the sadness from my heart. Yes, I wanted to start helping clean it up but it's a different time and place in my life and I must move forward and not look back. God would not want me to do that.

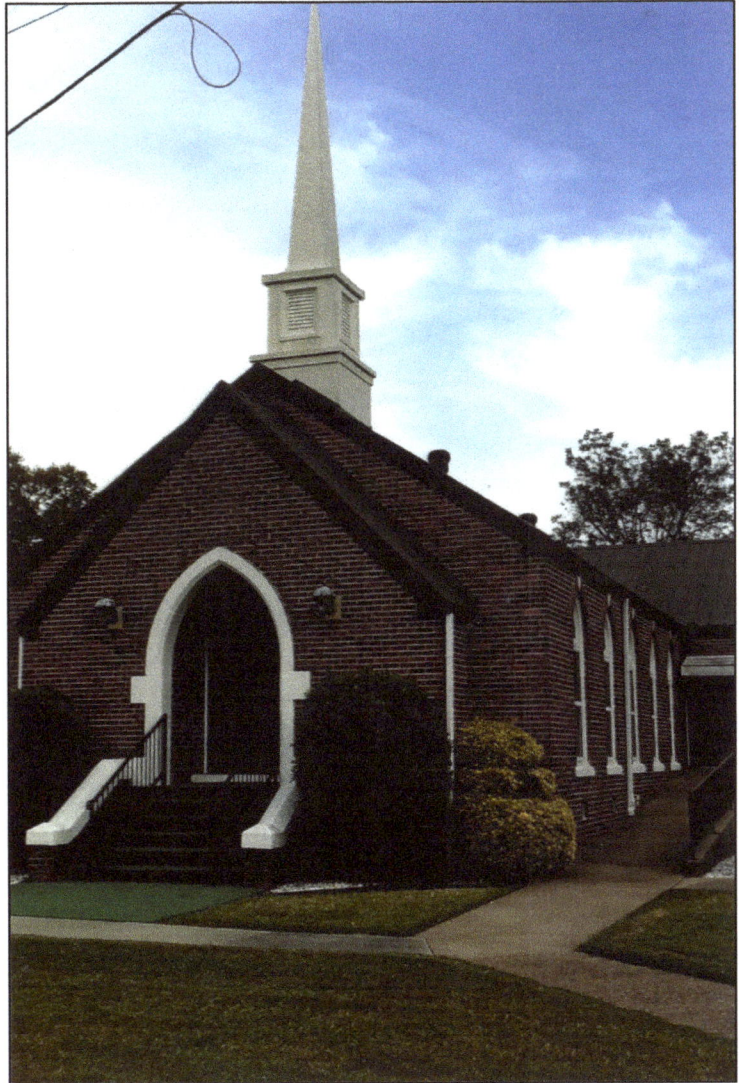

We were in the church by 11:00 AM and the service was starting. The Pastor, Bob Wheeler, took a moment, came to our pew and introduced himself. Joiner is very fortunate to have such a friendly, godly man leading them in Christ. A few people were there from my childhood days and the service was extra special with the youth group performing and the congregation singing all the old songs which included "Trust and Obey" and "Softly and Tenderly." Lunch was served (barbecue) in the fellowship hall, which I think was prepared by the members. There was an extended program after lunch scheduled with special music, history of the church and sharing of memories.

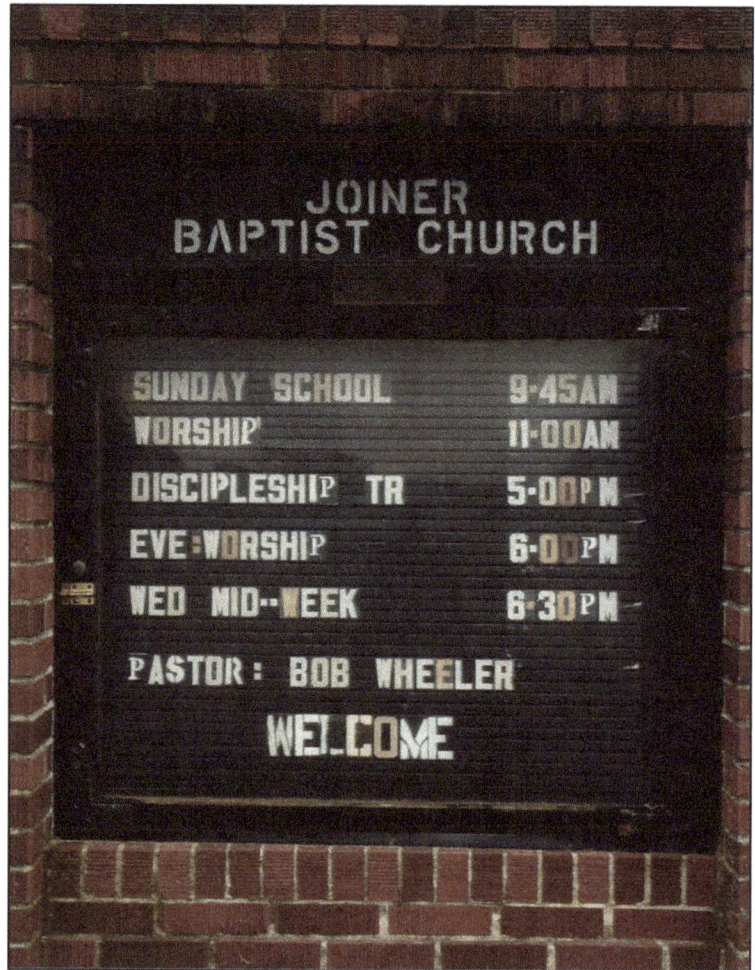

Eddie and I did not stay for lunch or the special program but my heart was so full of joy. Just seeing the beautiful church and the loving people brought back so many fulfilling memories. Pastor Bob Wheeler loves this church and the people. He is a happy and encouraging leader. I wish I lived closer so I could come more often. We live in Murfreesboro, Tennessee, and it is 550 miles round trip—so worth it!

Thank you First Baptist Church, Joiner, Arkansas, for a beautiful Moment in Time.

"I am able to do all things through him who strengthens me."

Philippians 4:13

Martha Lloyd Cooke

My writing journey commenced in 1999 with a few short stories and a couple of poems. Through the years, I have added an abundance of true stories and poetry about my family and friends, and also stories reflecting my Christian faith. Along with these writings, I have included many pictures that will hopefully help the reader understand my written words.

My hope is that you, the reader, will close "my book of life" with a happy feeling and be a little more blessed. Who knows? Maybe you will want to write *your* life story. Don't compare yourself to others. Just be yourself and take your heart out of the box, and start that journey!

"Have I not commanded you? Be strong and courageous. Do not be terrified; do not be discouraged, for the Lord your God will be with you wherever you go."

Joshua 1:9

www.ingramcontent.com/pod-product-compliance
Lightning Source LLC
Chambersburg PA
CBHW040318100426

42811CB00012B/1474

* 9 7 8 1 6 2 8 8 0 1 9 3 4 *